ORTHO'S All About

Landscape
Construction Basics

Meredith® Books
Des Moines, Iowa

Ortho® Books
An imprint of Meredith® Books

Ortho's All About Landscape Construction Basics

Editor: Larry Erickson
Art Director: Tom Wegner
Contributing Writer: Martin Miller
Copy Chief: Catherine Hamrick
Copy and Production Editor: Terri Fredrickson
Contributing Copy Editor: Steve Hallam
Contributing Proofreaders: Kathy Eastman, Ray Kast,
  Jay Lamar
Technical Reviewer: Ralph Selzer
Indexer: Donald Glassman
Electronic Production Coordinator: Paula Forest
Editorial and Design Assistants: Kathleen Stevens,
  Karen Schirm
Contributing Editorial Assistants: Janet Anderson,
  Colleen Johnson
Production Director: Douglas M. Johnston
Book Production Managers: Pam Kvitne,
  Marjorie J. Schenkelberg

**Additional Editorial Contributions from
  Art Rep Services**
Director: Chip Nadeau
Designer: lk Design
Photo Editor: Nancy South
Writer: Gary Branson
Illustrators: Shawn Wallace, John Teisberg

Meredith® Books
Editor in Chief: James D. Blume
Design Director: Matt Strelecki
Managing Editor: Gregory H. Kayko

Director, Sales & Marketing, Retail: Michael A. Peterson
Director, Sales & Marketing, Special Markets:
  Rita McMullen
Director, Sales & Marketing, Home & Garden Center
  Channel: Ray Wolf
Director, Operations: George A. Susral

Vice President, General Manager: Jamie L. Martin

Meredith Publishing Group
President, Publishing Group: Christopher M. Little
Vice President, Consumer Marketing & Development:
  Hal Oringer

Meredith Corporation
Chairman and Chief Executive Officer: William T. Kerr
Chairman of the Executive Committee: E.T. Meredith III

Photographers
(Photographers credited may retain copyright ©
  to the listed photographs.)
Liz Ball/Positive Images: 65 (bottom)
Gary Branson: 9 (BR)
Bob Braun: 10 (top)
Karen Bussolini/Positive Images: 63 (top)
Shelley Hawes/Decisive Moment Photography: 10 (BL), 21
Margaret Hensel: 40 (top)
John North Holtorf: Cover
Jerry Howard/Positive Images: 4 (top, bottom), 7 (top),
  10 (BR), 11 (top, bottom), 12, 32 (top), 33 right and CL,
  35 (top, center), 54 (left), 55 (top, BR), 59 (bottom)
Ivan Massar/Positive Images: 32 (bottom)
Robert Perron: 9 (top), 42 (top), 60 (left)

All of us at Ortho® Books are dedicated to providing you
with the information and ideas you need to enhance your
home and garden. We welcome your comments and
suggestions about this book. Write to us at:
  Meredith Corporation
  Ortho Books
  1716 Locust St.
  Des Moines, IA 50309–3023

If you would like more information on other Ortho
products, call 800-225-2883 or visit us at www.ortho.com

Note to the Readers: Due to differing conditions, tools,
and individual skills, Meredith Corporation assumes no
responsibility for any damages, injuries suffered, or losses
incurred as a result of following the information published
in this book. Before beginning any project, review the
instructions carefully, and if any doubts or questions remain,
consult local experts or authorities. Because codes and
regulations vary greatly, you always should check with
authorities to ensure that your project complies with all
applicable local codes and regulations. Always read and
observe all of the safety precautions provided by
manufacturers of any tools, equipment, or supplies,
and follow all accepted safety procedures.

The sweeping curves of a patio, walls, and pool convey a sense of rhythm and formal order in this private yard. Well-planned foliage accents the masonry design.

This informal patio is bordered by shrubbery and shaded by mature trees. A patio storage shed can hold a barbecue grill and other unused patio equipment, keeping the patio clean and uncluttered.

OUTDOOR SPACES, LIVING ROOMS

Think of your landscape as an outdoor room. Approach its design as you would the rooms inside your home. You'll be making "living" rooms in your backyard—for gatherings, entertainment, gardening, and children's play. Like interior design, landscape construction unifies the practical uses of space with elements that express your personality.

Good landscaping also increases the appeal and value of your home, and a well-planned landscape can even save you money—later additions are likely to cost less if you prepare for them as you build your first structures.

Nowhere is the importance of landscaping more evident than on a new construction site. The bare terrain and absence of personal expression leaves it looking unfinished and incomplete, like an unframed picture.

But resist the urge to dive right in and start building your new landscape immediately. You'll enjoy the process (and the final result) substantially more with a little preparation. This book will guide you through some basic planning steps, offering suggestions in the first chapter about planning, budgeting, and design tools that will make your landscape livable (and perhaps less costly).

In succeeding chapters, you'll find advice on tools and techniques, construction materials, and basic principles for building fences, walls, decks, patios, and other landscape structures.

Whether you're starting from scratch or renovating a landscape that simply isn't "you" or useful any more, this helpful information will meet your needs.

PLANNING AND DESIGN

To ensure minimum frustration and maximum enjoyment of your new landscape, you'll need to do some planning. Here are factors to consider: how you will use the space, how complex the structures are, your skill level, the time you have, your materials, and your landscape budget.

The photos on the opposite page offer excellent opportunities to compare some of these factors. The upper photo shows a very formal and expansive patio with space to entertain large groups. The circular pool—defined by a 3-tiered wall—lends an interesting focal point to the overall design. Masonry materials add color and texture, while the shrubbery calls to mind an English estate garden. This patio was designed with an eye toward permanence and visual impact, but with little concern for economy. The space conveys the feel of professional design and execution; however, planning

and executing such a project might well be beyond the scope of the average homeowner.

In the lower photo, a simple slab is adequate for handling the entertainment and leisure requirements of the homeowner. The design is uncomplicated but inviting and the space is large enough for extended family groups to have cookouts or conversation. Such a project's costs of design and materials are well within most family budgets; the cost is further reduced because this simple project is within the construction abilities of the average homeowner.

Both patios will serve their intended purposes, both are attractive and useful additions to their respective homes, and both have been planned by homeowners who paid careful attention to their individual needs, abilities, and budgets.

FORM AND FUNCTION

These homemade stepping stones show that concrete doesn't have to be dull. They invite you into the multicolored flower garden. Flagstone is as functional, but the look of the path would be different.

Your first thoughts about your landscape are likely to be about structures—a deck, privacy fence, or garden path. But before you finalize your plans, examine the functions each structure performs and think about the materials that will get the look you want.

MATERIALS FOR EFFECT

An unpainted fence provides privacy and a natural looking backdrop for the garden. The central brick column with its old-time lamppost adds a touch of quaintness to this naturalized setting.

If basic security is all you need, a chain link fence will fill the bill. But if you want wind and noise protection too, a wooden privacy fence is a better choice. It will give you security, privacy, and a windbreak all in one handsome package. Wood adds color, texture, and warmth, as well.

WALLS: Solid walls of brick or stone do more than stand up to the battering elements. They also convey a valid sense of permanence and stability. A brick or stone wall beside a garden bed creates an interesting interplay between the open space of your lawn and colorful plantings. A dry-set or mortared stone retaining wall can tame a slope, making a level place for your patio.

PATHS: A walkway works on two planes: It unites, leading from one area to another; and it separates, one side from the other—lawn from garden, for example.

Different materials will have strikingly different effects. Concrete gets the job done, but brick or pavers add beauty and character to the pathway. Wood chips, gravel, or flagstone have a rustic nature that settles comfortably on a wooded setting.

DECKS AND PATIOS: These are outdoor rooms at modest cost. If your gatherings are limited to family, a satellite structure—such as an outdoor dining area with sunken seating or a screened gazebo—may suffice.

If you need a deck for entertaining, build it large enough for comfort. And for comfort in the sun, plan for a shade structure over part of your deck or patio.

OBSTACLES

Your projects may all be smooth sailing, but be prepared to brave the climate and cost that may force you to alter course. If your summers are short, you may need to plan an enclosure for entertaining in cold weather. Look to local materials to avoid high prices. For example, where native stone is abundant, a stone retaining wall may be less expensive than natural timber. Don't base your plan on budget alone. Balance budget, structures, and materials to meet your needs.

Latticework on this canopy tones down the massive character of its posts and beams. A canopy makes a great addition to a deck, providing privacy and partial shade.

LISTS, LISTS, LISTS

Landscape construction involves a certain amount of list making, and there's no better time to start than now.

■ Begin with a list of activities you and your family want to enjoy. Then list structures and improvements that meet those needs.

■ List amenities—such as lighting, outlets, and gas lines—that will increase the comfort and usefulness of your new outdoor space. Including these early in the planning stages allows you to install utility lines during construction, rather than as costly add-ons.

■ List all modifications you want to make to your landscape. At each stage, your lists will include actions needed to make things happen. List-making can help you enjoy the process of transforming your landscape and can keep you on schedule and within budget.

Color unifies the elements in this design. Simple built-in benches and lattice panels break the horizontal plane, and colorful flowers keep the plan from looking plain.

EVALUATE THE SITE

GRADING FOR DRAINAGE

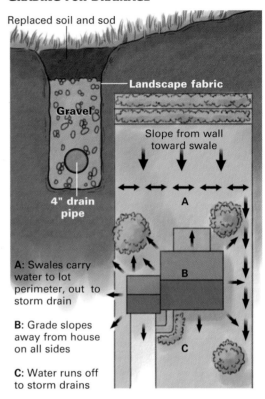

Replaced soil and sod

Landscape fabric

Gravel

4" drain pipe

Slope from wall toward swale

A

B

C

A: Swales carry water to lot perimeter, out to storm drain

B: Grade slopes away from house on all sides

C: Water runs off to storm drains

SITE PROBLEMS

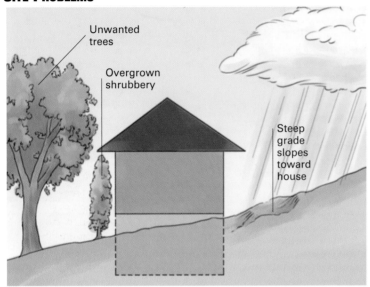

Unwanted trees

Overgrown shrubbery

Steep grade slopes toward house

Don't rush to build a deck or patio without taking stock of problems on your property. Improper drainage can ruin your carefully planned structures. Overgrown plants can hide them or bring more shade than you need.

One of the first things to do in planning your landscape is to evaluate your site. After a rain, do neighborhood kids come by to marvel at the eroded canyon or to play in the lake that covers your lawn? Are trees providing shade or just blocking a view? Or is the view undesirable anyway? How about street noise and privacy?

All of these factors—and how you deal with them—can determine where you put your deck, garden, or the children's play area.

List any problems that need correcting, including those you may have to work around. List assets, too: The existing features that add to the potential of your landscape. Post these lists beside your desk and refer to them often as you ponder your landscape construction plans. Every project should account for the assets and the pitfalls of your property. Give priority to projects that will add to your list of assets and reduce the list of problems.

SHADE AND SOIL

At the most basic level, every property has two definite qualities: light and a surface. Landscape design manipulates these qualities.

CAST SHADOWS: Add trees, overhangs, and other plants and structures to shade a sunlit deck or patio. An arbor or latticework with climbing roses creates and shades a private spot without blocking the breeze.

STOP EROSION: A common problem on steep slopes and sites with sandy soil, erosion can be checked with retaining walls or heavy-rooted groundcovers that hold the soil. Grade improper drainage so you have gradual, uninterrupted slopes away from structures.

ANALYZE DIRT: The type of soil you have can affect major landscape decisions.

■ **LOOSE, SANDY LOAM** absorbs and drains well, is good for plantings, and is easy to grade. It is subject to erosion and does not compact; you'll need to set posts in concrete.

■ **SILTED SOIL** is easy to dig and to compact, but posts for wooden fences exposed to wind will need to be set in concrete.

■ **CLAY** is compact and sheds water so easily that runoff is a problem. Fix it with grading or with drains to storm sewers or catch basins.

CHANGE THE VIEW

Open up your landscape by removing trees or shrubbery that block pleasant views. Remove or repair unsound and unsightly sheds and other structures. Privacy screens, fences, trees, and other plantings will hide unwanted views. And weed out anything that's overgrown or makes a natural mess. Replace out-of-control shrubs with low-growing varieties and pod-bearing trees with more desirable species.

Increase your privacy and reduce noise with trees or high, thick hedges. Privacy screens and fences can also help buffer noise and block visibility from the street.

CONSIDER THE NEIGHBORHOOD

The adage "no man is an island" applies as well to your house and landscape. Major changes to your property—especially to the front or other public areas—will affect the entire neighborhood. It's good to keep that in mind as you plan. But don't worry; you don't have to lose your individuality. Your landscape can be outstanding without standing out. If you maintain the harmony of the overall neighborhood, you will enhance the appeal of not only your home but your neighbors' homes as well.

Walk your block and make notes of any unifying elements, especially on properties adjacent to yours. If the neighborhood style is consistent, what can you do to maintain it? If it's a stylistic patchwork, attempt to minimize the hodge-podge.

For example, some neighborhoods are built without obvious boundaries, creating an open, sweeping effect. Tall privacy fences or hedges would interrupt the continuity. Other neighborhoods convey a strong regional style, and you can enhance that effect with native plantings and local materials. You and your neighbors may want to get together to coordinate plantings that hide the property lines and complement all of your homes.

Don't overlook the streetscape. Plant parking strips and choose streetside trees that complement the style of the neighborhood.

Before you start planting or building close to your property lines, be sure you know where they actually are. If you aren't sure, invest in a survey. Money spent now will save costly disagreements in the future. Also, check with your local government's building department about setback restrictions that limit the distance between structures and property boundaries.

For a fee, many real estate agents and landscape designers will perform a site inspection and offer useful advice on projects that will fit into your neighborhood.

BLEND WITH THE ENVIRONMENT

Although the structures and other elements of your plans will be determined largely by how you want to use your landscape, they should blend with both the architecture of your house and the configurations of the land.

For example, the architecture of a 1920s four-square home might be better reflected in a flagstone patio than in a concrete slab. Brick in sand can complement the geometric lines of a modern single-story house. Scalloped trim is most at home with the gingerbread of early American or Victorian. Modern masonry patios and wood decks are compatible with a wide variety of styles, and a gazebo or an overhead stained an attractive color fits well in any environment.

Also consider the lay of the land, your climate, and the natural vegetation. Then create a style that reflects what is natural. Uneven terrain lends itself to simple and informal lines; a large lot will let you use bolder strokes.

Choose materials that are native to your area. You'll save on shipping costs, and the additions to your landscape will appear as though nature helped you put them there. Redwood, for example, is less expensive in the western states, cypress in the south, and cedar in the north from west to east.

A flagstone walk and potted plantings invite you to this portico. The rear wall increases the accent quality of the portico, ensures privacy, and provides screening from the wind.

DESIGN PRINCIPLES

One of the quickest ways to develop an understanding of design—and to get you going in a direction that reflects your personality—is to split the subject into two categories: formal and informal.

FORMAL AND INFORMAL

The terms apply to lifestyle as well as appearance. You probably know immediately into which camp you fit.

OBVIOUS ORDER: Formal design is characterized by straight lines, right angles, geometric shapes, and even-numbered groupings. It creates a sense of regularity and symmetry. A square deck or patio with rectangular brick patterns suggests formality. So do pairs—trees or other plantings, decorative items, and structural elements.

CASUAL COMFORT: You can recognize informal designs, on the other hand, by their curved lines, irregular shapes, and groupings of odd-numbered items. Informality is about taking delight in the unexpected. A cottage-style home may be the perfect spot for curving bedlines, and even your deck can incorporate elements of informal line.

Examine the kinds of landscapes you like; you'll probably find that your tastes fall generally into one category or another. Then maintain that style in your paving patterns, fences, and patio design.

GET EVERYONE INVOLVED

Your final plan should have something in it for everyone, so get the whole family together to develop the goals. A vegetable garden and raised flower bed will serve the family member who has a green thumb. Children will need a play area, perhaps with a sand box and swings, and teenagers will want a stretch of lawn for touch football. Parents might want a sheltered, shaded place to get away to, in addition to the deck or patio. Plan enough space for each area— for decks especially; examine family traffic patterns, and make sure your improvements reflect actual use.

The geometry of the borders brings a pleasant, curved contrast to the peaked roof. Everything looks neat and orderly. Shrubbery and flower beds were designed with the help of a landscape professional.

The arched entry gates create a novel, gothic effect in these garden fences. The lattice fencing permits light and air to flow through while ensuring privacy.

LIVING COLOR

Colorful accents spice up your landscape. A fruit tree in bloom or a bed of spring flowers will put an end to winter's dreariness, and lush greenery with splashes of flowers will take you through the summer. Don't stop there. Extend the palette into fall with brilliant autumn-colored trees. And the form of many vines and perennials, as well as evergreens, can brighten winter views.

FOCAL POINTS

When your eye follows an imaginary line and focuses on an object, it is following an *axis* and coming to rest on a *focal point*.

Axes in formal landscapes will be linear, with garden sculptures and formal plantings placed where the lines terminate. Informal design styles are less direct and imply the lines of sight with pathways and paving patterns, night lighting, and natural elements.

A focal point can be any feature of the finished landscape—a rose arbor, a flowering tree, or a fountain. Focal points can be as small as a single planting or as large as a deck or an arched bridge over a pond.

Sometimes the obvious focal point is beyond your yard—a hill, valley, or sweeping vista. Why compete? Plan your landscape to frame and complement a good view.

POINTS OF VIEW

Perspectives are points of view, and in the landscape they vary greatly, depending on where you stand. Each has a different feeling. Views from above, such as from an elevated deck, can offer a sense of unity, space, and detachment. A level perspective, as from paths or doorways, connects you to the surroundings. Views from below—standing in a sunken garden, for example—can feel cozy and secure to some, oppressive to others.

Always test perspectives before you build. A ladder or an upper-story window can give you a sense of the view from an elevated deck. From the back door, you can imagine how a patio will stretch your home interior into the outdoors. And you might decide against that extra-tall deck if you know ahead of time that it will provide a splendid bird's-eye view of the neighbor's roadster restoration that has been hidden by a hedge for years.

FORCING PERSPECTIVE

Objects appear to be smaller and less detailed in the distance. You can utilize a tool of the design trade called "forcing perspective"—causing objects to seem farther away than they really are. It's easy: Put small plants in the background and large varieties in the front, or taper garden beds and walkways to the rear; you will create the impression that a shallow yard is longer than it is.

The curve of the walk conceals the area beyond and invites the visitor to enter and explore the unseen garden.

PUBLIC AND PRIVATE SPACES

Public space becomes more private by the wide expanse of front lawn, mature trees, and carefully arranged foundation plantings of shrubs and flowers.

For landscape planning purposes, decide whether the affected area of your yard is public or private. The public yard is any area that's apparent to public view—usually the front lawn only, but on some lots that includes side yards, too. The private yard is reserved for recreation and entertainment— normally the backyard and side yards that are screened from public view.

Both areas have different functions and personalities; you will want to design each with a slightly different eye. They can contain the same basic elements—walkways, trees, lawn, shrubs, planting beds, and entrances— but their purposes are different.

THE PUBLIC YARD

When real estate agents refer to curb appeal, they are talking about the public yard. Your challenge is to choose structures and materials that maximize curb appeal and complement the neighborhood.

Take a tour of neighborhoods you like. Assess the designs of other properties. What appeals to you? Take notes and photos, or make sketches for future reference. Clip magazine articles that contain ideas you want to use. Visit parks and arboretums; make your own gallery of complementary features and put them in a file.

LOOK FOR COMPLEMENTS: Your landscape choices are limited only by your imagination and budget. Even the driveway can be made attractive. Concrete can contain curves and patterns or can be tinted with colors to complement your color scheme. Bricks and pavers add a touch of elegance. So does a cut-stone retaining wall with planters overflowing with your favorite flowers.

Don't rule out fences for the public yard, but don't enclose yourself in a stockade with a high privacy fence. Complement your neighborhood (and your own property). Chain link will provide security and won't obstruct the view, and a coat of paint will dress up its strictly functional appearance. Or plant twining vines or climbing roses for a living wall of color. Painted low-cut picket fences are excellent accents for bungalows or cottage-style decor. Wrought iron accents colonial and Victorian styles.

LOW-COST OPTIONS: Use low-cost timbers for retaining walls instead of more expensive stone, interlocking blocks, or brick and mortar.

You can enhance masonry inexpensively with built-in flower boxes. Formalize them with a rigid pattern or go informal with random placement. Either way, you add enticing accents and reduce the hard, monolithic image of the masonry surface.

Small improvements in a public yard make great strides toward improving curb appeal. Decorative, low-voltage lighting makes the entry more inviting. Distinctive brass or wooden house numbers, or a brightly-painted or hand-carved oak door with sidelights can also make an impact on curb appeal without affecting your budget.

The patio in this private yard offers space for entertaining or a quiet weekend brunch. The interplay of color and shapes suggests that the homeowners paid careful attention to their plantings.

THE PRIVATE YARD

What determines your approach to backyard planning is how you will use it. This is your personal preserve, a place where you can invite the whole gang over or quietly get away from it all.

DIVIDE AND CONQUER: Depending on the size of your household, you may have to share this so-called private space. You could carve it into personal parcels, but you can be more methodical.

■ **BEST WISHES:** Begin with wish lists, one per family member. Write down things you've always wanted (set costs aside for now.) Compile a master list of everyone's wishes.

■ **NEEDS ASSESSMENT:** Next, examine what you and your family really need. Make a family master list and compare the two. There are probably several things on your needs list ("hide the garbage cans," for example) that aren't among your wishes.

■ **COMPROMISE:** Make one list from the two, then begin a reality check against your budget. And note how many wish lists share a common desire. A large or expensive feature—a pool, for example—might be more viable if everyone wants it.

If large projects dominate your plans, sometimes smaller ones will do. A small deck, for instance, is more affordable, especially if it can be built in phases over time.

AREAS FOR SPECIFIC NEEDS: Establish a definite area for specific uses of your yard and separate them with hedges, planting beds, or low fences. Provide pathways between distinct areas of use. Paths link areas and make excellent dividers, too.

Look for relationships between the areas and plan their locations so they don't compete with one another. Children's play areas, for example, should be situated so their joyful noise does not interfere with your enjoyment of the deck or patio. But keep them within sight for safety and supervision.

If you frequently entertain large groups, consider supplementing your deck or patio with satellite retreats. These are spots around the yard where smaller groups can gather:
■ a sunken seating area with a fire pit
■ a small flagstone patio in the garden
■ a picnic table and umbrella
Satellites offer options, including the option to build a moderately sized deck even though you sometimes entertain large groups.

Separate your private yard from the rest of the world with hedges, fences, walls, and privacy screens. But if you plan other large construction or excavation, don't build fences first; you'll need access for heavy equipment.

TEST DRIVE: Take a trial run with your deck design or any other large addition. Outline the proposed area with spray paint or rope. Arrange all the pieces of furniture and any accents you plan to use, such as potted plants. Have the family move about this new "room." A 4-foot table may require 9 feet of space when surrounded by people and chairs.

THE NEIGHBORS' VIEWS

Consider how your landscape plans will affect your neighbors' views. Ask for permission to walk through their yards and visualize how they will be affected by your project. If a proposed structure will affect their view, consider relocating it. Build fences or privacy screens so they are as attractive from the neighbor's side as from yours.

PLANNING LIKE A PRO

Designating space for specific uses, such as play, entertainment, or gardening, is a giant step. At this point, you've decided which projects you will include in your new landscape and you have a pretty good idea of where you'll put them. Now it's time to put the plan on paper.

To draw working plans, you will need graph paper and a ruler, each with the same scale (¼ inch is a good choice), tracing paper, masking tape, pencils, and erasers.

BASE MAP

Start with a base map—an outline drawing of the permanent features of your lot. It will show the house, other structures, walkways, driveway, trees, and major plantings.

To begin, buy, borrow, or rent a 100-foot rule to measure your lot and house. Transfer these measurements onto your paper. Be sure the drawing is to scale and locates each item accurately, including distances between structures and from structures to the property's boundaries.

Show locations of windows, doors, hose bibs, and electrical outlets. Use dotted lines for any buried cable (check with your utility companies to be sure). You may find that your proposed patio site covers a utility line, which will make future access difficult and costly. **SHORTCUTS:** You can shorten the base-map step somewhat by using a plot map of your property, which you may find in the documents you received when you bought your home. Plot maps are also available from your local government records office. Or you can commission a survey (a necessity if your plan includes extensive grading), but expect to pay a few hundred dollars. In either case, mark the locations of trees, storage sheds, buried cables, and major plantings.

BUBBLE DIAGRAM

Next you'll make a bubble diagram—and you may end up making several. Tape a sheet of tracing paper over your base map. Using your final list of design ideas, draw circled areas for each project in its proposed location—your deck, patio, storage locations, and flower beds.

Include ideas for walkways and paths—everything that will be new. If you make mistakes or change your mind, erase or use a new sheet of tracing paper. No one is going to critique your artwork. Indicate problem areas on your bubble diagram, too—areas where you need to open up the view or grade for proper drainage.

When your bubble diagram is done, you may want to consult a landscape architect or planner. The trained eyes of a professional can spot design flaws or potential problems and may well be worth the expense.

CONTROLLING COSTS

There are two factors to consider when analyzing costs—the initial outlay and the costs of long-term maintenance. Costs cut initially may lead to greater costs over the life of the project.

Here are some tips that can help balance the two concerns, as well as your budget.

■ Sometimes lower-grade materials will fill the bill—especially if they won't be visible. Lumber is a prime example. Use heartwood of cedar, redwood, or cypress for deck structures or fence posts that will come into contact with the ground. Cheaper grades are fine for ledgers, joists, and above-ground structural members. Splurge a little on the decking and the rails. Pressure-treated wood is cheaper still, but also comes in various grades. Use fully treated lumber for ground contact. Your dealer can advise you which grade will best serve each purpose.

■ Never scrimp on fasteners. You won't save money in the long run. Use only galvanized, stainless steel, aluminum, or corrosion-resistant fasteners.

■ A fence or privacy screen may benefit your neighbor as much as you. Visit your neighbor, explain your project, and ask if he or she is willing to share the costs and the benefits as well.

■ Ask for discounts. Take your plan to your supply dealer and see if you can get a contractor's discount if you buy the entire package. Contractors routinely receive 10 to 20 percent discounts for large projects. If you cannot obtain a discount, shop home centers for the best prices.

■ Most lumber and fencing material is cut in even multiples—4-, 6-, and 8-foot lengths. To contain costs, waste, and labor, avoid erecting a 5½-foot fence.

■ Make your plans as detailed as possible. Details will help you make accurate estimates of the time each part of the project will take and will allow any contractors you hire to accurately bid their work.

BUBBLE PLAN

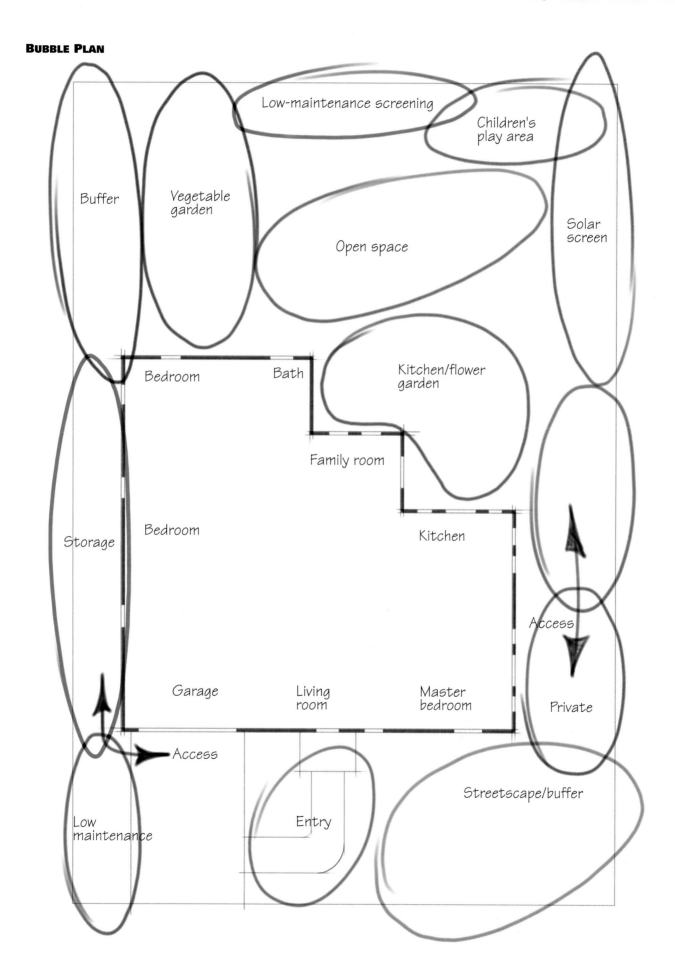

FINALLY, YOUR MASTER PLAN

Now that you're sure where everything in your new landscape will be, it's time to get a little more specific.

First, you'll need to make a master plan on another sheet of tracing paper. A master plan lets you make sure everything fits just where you want it and gives you a bird's eye preview of your new landscape. Your master plan will be the foundation for detailed drawings and will provide a basis for ballpark cost estimates.

Lay a piece of tracing paper over your base map and trace the outlines of your house and other existing features. Now make rough drawings of the new structures you will build, using your bubble diagrams to help you decide where everything will go.

STRUCTURES FIRST

Start with the structural elements—the decks, patios, parking areas, landings, and pathways. Designers call this *hardscape*. Play with different shapes and lines, but don't waste time drawing meticulous plans.

Instead, explore ideas freely. If a square-cornered deck doesn't look just right—or if it doesn't fit the space—try another shape. If a straight walk to your goldfish pond is too direct or needs to follow the contours of the land, bend it. This is still a time for experimentation, and it's easily changed on paper. Keep your sketches close to scale, but don't get stuck on any one area too long. You will figure out the details in the next step. Keep "the big picture" in mind as you work.

PLANTS AND TREES

Once you draw the hardscape lines, add lawn and planting areas with their bedlines. Because they are used as separations, bedlines shape two adjacent spaces at one time. You can make them formal and geometric or curve them with a flowing informality.

Next, sketch with circles any trees you plan to plant, referring to your bubble diagram to remind you of any view you want to frame or areas that need privacy or shade.

Finally, put labels on your sketches and include them on the floor plan drawing of your house. Make one last check on the relationships each area has with the interior of your home. You may have forgotten that you had planned to remove a tree to open up a view or add high shrubbery to make an interior room more private.

TAKE A WALK-THROUGH

Now take your plan outside and walk it through your property. Make sure you haven't forgotten anything. Are all the access routes workable? Have you accounted for screening? Do the axis lines call attention to the right focal points? Can you move a structure within your plan to a spot where you won't have to excavate—without botching the rest of your design?

Even if you intend to build your landscape in stages over a period of years, the master plan will keep your design unified, both now and in the future.

HIGH-TECH HELP

Computerized landscape-design programs take the pencil (and eraser) out of planning. They're easy to use, flexible, and can speed your progress from base plan to final design. One of a computer's more appealing features is deletion—an electronic eraser that allows you to change your design without redrawing it.

The features are slick: Programs calculate dimensions of each of your proposed structures and areas of use. Most programs have a number of symbols for trees and shrubs, as well as elements such as furniture, pools, and patios. Some will even create side elevations and three-dimensional views of your plan. Others can prepare material lists and cost estimates.

Check your home improvement center, too. Many offer computer design services. If you're not familiar with computers, you can take your rough drawings (including dimensions) and the store's staff will computerize your project and produce a materials list and cost estimates. Ask for extra copies—your local government building department will need them when you apply for permits.

FINISHED SITE PLAN

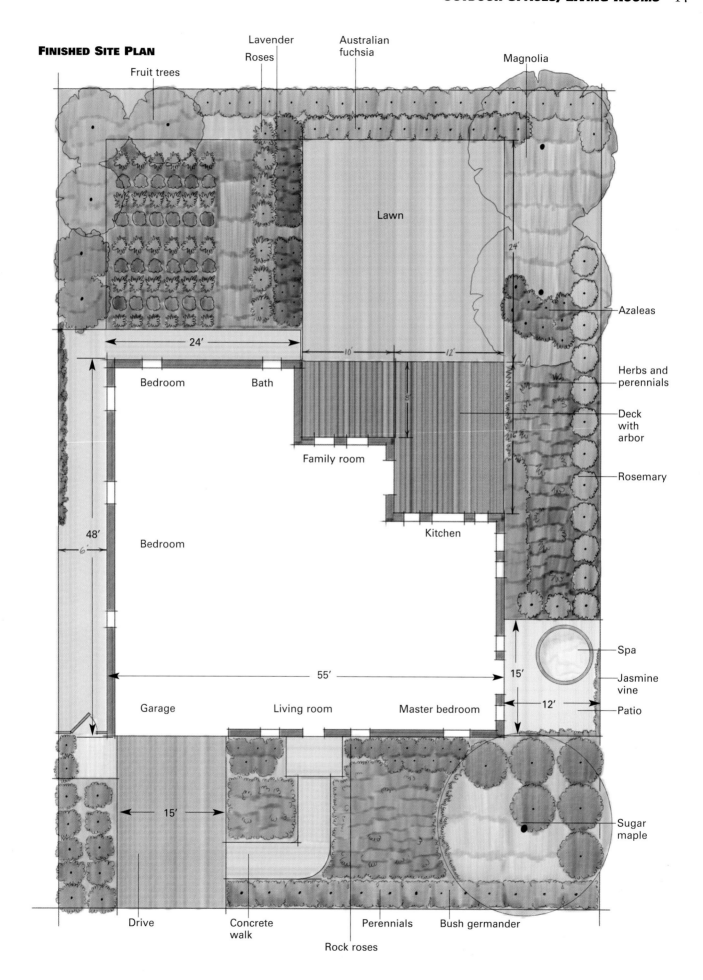

Lavender

Roses

Australian fuchsia

Magnolia

Fruit trees

Lawn

Azaleas

24'

10'

12'

Bedroom

Bath

Herbs and perennials

Deck with arbor

8'

Family room

Rosemary

48'

6'

Bedroom

Kitchen

55'

15'

Spa

Jasmine vine

Garage

Living room

Master bedroom

12'

Patio

15'

Sugar maple

Drive

Concrete walk

Perennials

Bush germander

Rock roses

DIMENSIONS AND DETAILS

A layout plan and working drawings will put the final touches on your design. A layout plan is an outline with overall dimensions. Working drawings show details for each structure you plan to build.

To make a layout plan, trace the outline of your house and all the hardscape. You won't need to show new plants or any you will remove, but do show trees and large shrubs that will remain.

LAYING THINGS OUT

Now for the dimension lines—they look like an "H" with the crossbar extending from one edge of a structure to the other. Use the illustration on page 17 as a guide. Dimension lines help keep your plan uncluttered. This is a time for precision; and if you can, conform your specifications to standard material sizes.

Some measurements are, by nature, approximate and will become exact (the exact length of a curving path, for example) only when your yard becomes a job site. Note approximations with a plus-or-minus (±) sign.

LAST CALL FOR CHANGES

Don't be afraid to adjust things as you go. A layout plan is a great place to bring your design to its ultimate refinement. Time spent now will make construction stages proceed much more smoothly later. A layout plan also allows you to get bids from contractors; then if costs force you to revise your design, you'll know exactly the effect of any changes.

Each structure will need a separate drawing that details its construction. You can hire a professional at this stage; if your plans are uncomplicated, you can sketch them out yourself or with the help of your contractor. Detailed drawings of a deck, for example would include footings, posts, posthole depths, and rails, and how each piece is fastened to another. A detailed drawing is the place to indicate materials, stain or paint colors, and other specifics of construction.

Finally, detailed drawings will help you decide how much of the work you want to do yourself and how much of it you will contract.

WRITTEN WORK DESCRIPTION

To help keep the building process organized, make a list of tasks by category. Arrange your written work description in the order that activities will be accomplished; then use it to develop a construction calendar or timeline.

Under each category, include all structures to which the work applies. For example, your patio slab and footings for the deck should both be listed under concrete work.

Here's a sample list that includes most common construction categories, a model of what your work description might look like:

SITE PREPARATION: Remove unwanted trees and shrubs; mark trees to be saved and "equipment off-limits" zones.

EXCAVATION: Dig deck footings, fence postholes, slab bases, and drainage solutions, if necessary.

CONCRETE WORK: Pour deck footings, fence postholes, slab bases, and footings for retaining wall.

MASONRY: Lay brick on the walkway, patio, and retaining wall.

ROUGH CARPENTRY: Build the deck, privacy fence, overhead, and storage shed.

ELECTRICAL WORK: Run lines and install breakers and outlets to deck and spa.

FINISH CARPENTRY: Install trim on the new entryway and lattice for the patio screen.

PAINT/STAIN: Stain deck and the new door; paint the storage shed and latticework.

SITE FINISHING: Seed new lawn areas, plant trees and new flower beds.

Finishing similar tasks within the same time frame will save time and money, and will keep the work on schedule.

SCHEDULING

There is a natural progression to construction projects. Use your written work description to establish the order in which you will proceed. Coordinate each stage so that all phases leading up to it are finished first. Bunch jobs together. If you have three projects that require footings, dig all the holes, have them inspected, and arrange to have them poured at the same time.

The work description will also give you cues for ordering materials. Materials that are prematurely delivered to the job site become obstacles and are subject to weathering and damage. Lumber that is stacked outdoors will absorb moisture and can shrink excessively after being put in place. Cement bags may be split by a careless worker, and the cement will harden in the bag when exposed to moisture.

Allow for weather delays. A heavy rain can create a muddy job site and make the lawn too soft for deliveries or excavation.

SHOULD YOU HIRE A CONTRACTOR?

DOING IT YOURSELF

The explosive growth of the do-it-yourself industry shows that many homeowners can handle all but the most extensive landscape projects. When you're deciding whether to do the work yourself or hire it out, consider these points:

■ **DON'T KID YOURSELF:** Weigh your skill level and experience against the scope of the project. You can do minor excavating with a post-hole digger or shovel. Patios and driveway slabs require heavy equipment. If your carpentry skills are weak, buy precut kits for sheds, gazebos, and privacy fencing.

■ **WILL FRIENDS HELP?** Many construction projects require at least two sets of hands when setting deck joists, lifting framing lumber into position on an overhead, or pouring and leveling concrete slabs.

■ **EMPOWERMENT:** Power tools save time. So does proper planning. Buy a power screwdriver if you don't have one. It will be a valuable addition to your tool kit. Rent a power miter box for corner cuts, and a reciprocating saw for cutting posts or timbers. Don't build fences until the major projects are completed, and have materials dropped next to the project. Anything you can do to reduce your labor will make the job more enjoyable.

■ **ADD IT UP:** What will your total costs be? Make sure your materials list is complete and get prices for everything. Add subcontractor bids for any work you will definitely contract—excavation or electrical wiring, for example. Include the cost of tools you'll have to buy or rent, as well as waste removal, permits, and inspections. Add these costs together and compare them with a general contractor's bid.

Are the savings large enough to warrant taking the project on? Even if the savings are small, remember that doing it yourself can be an enjoyable and rewarding experience.

CONTRACTING THE JOB

Now that you've decided what projects to contract, how do you find a contractor? Friends and neighbors are good for references. So are local garden shops. But don't work with any contractor whose references you have not checked.

You may also need to enlist the services of landscape professionals such as:

■ **LANDSCAPE ARCHITECTS:** They completely design and plan your landscape, producing detailed drawings, plans, and written work descriptions. They will also supervise the construction.

■ **LANDSCAPE DESIGNERS:** They will assist you with the design of your project and will provide drawings for its general design, but not those requiring construction details.

■ **LANDSCAPE CONTRACTORS:** These builders have particular expertise in landscape construction.

Some firms describe themselves as "Designers and Builders." Such firms have professional architects, designers, and builders on their staff.

The best way to find a reputable design professional is through the satisfied references of friends and family. Ask at work or parties: Anyone who has a new landscape will be happy to talk about it and the professionals who made it happen.

■ **REFERENCES:** Once you've selected a group of contractors, ask each one for job references, and check them. Visit one of their job sites and inspect the quality of the work.

■ **BIDS:** Get several bids, and be wary of any that are significantly higher or lower than the average. The bids of reputable contractors bidding for the same work with the same materials should be close.

■ **CONTRACTS AND DOCUMENTS:** Get everything in writing—everything. Read the contract carefully, and insert any information that you feel is needed. If you have any uncertainty, have your lawyer review the documents before you sign. The contract should specify:

■ The work to be done.
■ Materials to be used.
■ A start date and completion schedule.
■ Procedure for making changes.
■ Stipulations that the contractor will obtain building permits and lien waivers.
■ Methods for resolving disputes.

Often required by local laws, your contractor should provide evidence of:

■ Licensing: showing he or she has met government standards to do the work.
■ Bonding: evidence that if the contractor fails to perform the work, a bonding company will pay another contractor to finish the job.
■ Insurance: liability for non-workers, workman's compensation for workers injured on the job.

FINAL PAYMENT

Before you make final payment, obtain signed lien waivers from the contractor for every subcontractor and supplier. You'll avoid liability in case the contractor fails to pay them.

When the job is completed, inspect it carefully. If anything looks questionable, make a note of it. Ask the contractor to do a walk-through with you, so you can point out problems; then both of you can see first hand what needs to be corrected. The contractor should either correct any problems or explain why they really aren't problems.

Many cities provide recourse for resolution of future problems—usually for a year. Check with your local building department. If problems arise, appeal first to the contractors involved, and allow a reasonable time for repairs. Then appeal to the professional associations to which they belong, or consult a lawyer.

LANDSCAPE BUILDER'S BASIC SKILLS

Some basic tools and techniques apply to all landscape projects. Building a concrete patio, for example, or any structure that has footings, requires some knowledge of working with concrete. You'll call on masonry techniques for mortared walls and walkways. And throughout your landscape work, you'll cut and measure constantly. In this section, you'll find a primer of the skills you need to get started.

TOOLS

If you have any experience with home and yard maintenance, you probably own most of the tools you need for landscape projects. If not, consider these suggestions:
■ Buy the best you can afford. Cheap tools wear out quickly, can be dangerous, and will cost you more in the long run.
■ Add a portable workbench and a 100-foot drop cord to your tool inventory.
■ Buy power tools with reinforced cords, ball or roller bearings, and double insulation to protect from electrical shock.
■ Garage sales and flea markets offer bargains on hand tools. But it's wise to purchase power tools new.
■ Mark your tools and don't leave them lying around your construction site.

SAFETY FIRST

Construction tools cut, pound, and grind. Flesh doesn't stand up well to that kind of treatment, so be safety-minded. Self defense makes sense. We recommend the following:
■ Wear heavy-soled work boots with over-the-ankle support to protect you from wayward nails and twisted missteps.
■ Wear durable gloves and denim jeans (or genuine construction togs, such as painter's pants) to protect your skin. Work clothes also have pockets to keep small tools at hand.
■ Wear goggles when sawing, hammering, or using power tools.
■ Use a dust mask or OSHA-approved respirator to let you breathe comfortably when spraying or sawing.
■ Plug all tools into outlets that are protected with ground fault circuit interrupters (GFCIs).
■ Keep a first-aid kit handy for minor injuries.
■ Wear a tool belt. You won't misplace tools and having them at hand saves time and energy.
■ Don't work with dull blades. They overwork the tool as well as the user—and they're dangerous.
■ Check before you dig. There's always a chance of running into utility lines if you don't find out where they are first. Most utility companies will send a locator quickly and free of charge.

RENTAL TOOL TIPS

Rent tools you won't use frequently, and be sure to ask the dealer for instructions about safe and proper use. To control rental costs, plan your job carefully. You'll save money if you have the work ready so the tool stays busy. Here's a list of tools commonly rented for landscape projects.

■ **EXCAVATION TOOLS:** transit or water level for checking a level grade, power auger for postholes, and a tractor with bucket for grading or spreading gravel base.
■ **MASONRY TOOLS:** soil compactor for bed preparation, concrete mixer, masonry saw, and electric jackhammer.
■ **CARPENTRY TOOLS:** power miter box for cutting corners, reciprocating saw for heavy timbers, pneumatic nailer, and a 100-foot tape.

Power nailers

Power tamper

Power auger

Concrete/masonry saw

Chain saw

Bull float

Corded and cordless drills

Handheld concrete saw

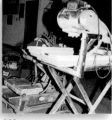
Wet saw

A construction adage states, "By the tools, you shall know the workman." Having the right tool makes the job easier and cuts labor time. Many expensive power tools are needed only for a single project, so shop a rental center to find these specialty items. To control rental charges, plan the work so you have the tool only long enough to do its job, and return it promptly when the work is finished.

GRADING AND EXCAVATION

CURING DRAINAGE PROBLEMS

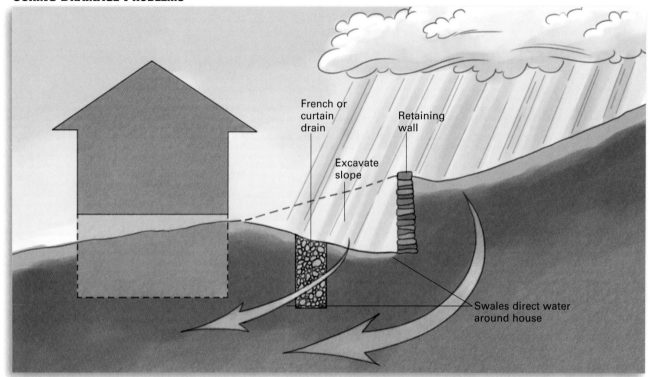

French or curtain drain

Retaining wall

Excavate slope

Swales direct water around house

Grading is simply removing surface earth. Excavation means removing earth below the grade.

Most grading for landscape projects will involve leveling the ground for lawn or patio areas, sloping the soil away from the house, and creating berms. Excavation will include cutting slopes for retaining walls and doing lots of digging—trenches for footings, holes for fence posts, and beds for walkways.

ORGANIZE YOUR WORK

Begin your rough grading and excavation before you start building decks, patios, or other structural items. Finish grading is usually done with hand rakes and can wait until just before you're ready to plant flower or shrub beds. Lay conduit for electrical lines before you pour the concrete.

CUT AND FILL

Minimize the amount of earth moved by balancing "cut and fill." Estimate the amount of earth needed to fill low spots and remove an equivalent amount from slopes that need leveling or drainage correction. You'll save time and money on hauling fill-dirt and you'll disturb fewer plantings

GET HELP FROM A PRO

Although you can do finish grading and many small excavations yourself, rough grading and major excavation call for earth-moving equipment. Even if you can do the work by hand, it may be more efficient to spend $500 to have it done all at once than to spend four weekends at hard labor. You'll free your time to work on things you can easily do yourself. Costs include an hourly equipment fee and an operator's expense—another reason for scheduling grading and excavation to be accomplished at the same time.

SITE PREPARATION

Extensive landscaping projects—especially those that require heavy equipment—call for some preliminary site preparation.
■ **PROTECT YOUR TREES:** Use flagging tape to mark trees you want to keep. Siltation fences keep displaced soil from covering root zones.
■ **LIMIT ACCESS:** Designate and mark heavy equipment access points. Barricade driveways against heavy equipment, which can crack the concrete.
■ **KEEP IT SAFE:** Barricade holes (even shallow excavations) and make sure tools are removed at the end of each work day.

DRAINAGE REMEDIES

Where will the runoff go? You need to answer that question before beginning any grading. Improper drainage can damage hardscape and plantings. It can cause concrete surfaces to become slick with mud, wash out flower beds, seep into basements, and crack foundations. Fortunately, almost any drainage problem can be fixed with one or more of these remedies:

POSITIVE DRAINAGE: Paved surfaces should slope slightly away from foundations and toward lower ground. Slope patio and concrete surfaces toward their edges, so water doesn't puddle on the patio. A slope of just 2 percent is adequate to move runoff. That's about 2 inches over a span of 8 feet.

SWALES: You can intercept water and direct it around objects with these gentle surface ditches. A swale must slope continuously and can be tiled or planted with grass. Water from a swale should empty on an open lawn—but never into the neighbor's yard. It is usually illegal and certainly inconsiderate to divert water so it flows onto adjacent properties.

FRENCH AND CURTAIN DRAINS: Easy to install, these are trenches with perforated pipe set in a gravel bed to carry water away from structures or low spots. See the instructions below.

DRY WELLS: These gravel-filled holes serve as outlets for water from other trenches. Typically 2 to 4 feet wide and 3 feet deep (check with local codes), they must be placed at least 10 feet from the house and covered with a concrete slab and planted soil. They are especially useful where water cannot be diverted to a storm sewer.

CATCH BASINS: These underground receptacles hold water from surface drains and direct it through underground pipes to storm sewers or other outlets. You can purchase pre-cast units at your materials outlet.

FOUNDATION DRAINAGE

If you have water in your basement, it may be caused by ground sloping toward the foundation. Here's an easy solution: Slope the soil next to the foundation away from the house for a distance of at least 4 feet. Bring in new soil as necessary. Lay landscape fabric over the slope. If you're going to plant the area, cut holes in the plastic for the plants. Decorative rock or wood chips will camouflage the plastic.

BUILDING A FRENCH OR CURTAIN DRAIN

The only difference between a French and a curtain drain is how their surfaces are finished. The gravel is left exposed over a French drain. A curtain drain is covered with soil and then planted.

To build either of these drains around the foundation of your house, excavate a 2-foot-wide trench parallel to—and about 2 feet away from—the wall. The trench should be as deep as the lowest leak and should slope ⅛ inch for every running foot.

The trench should terminate in a dry well or storm sewer, or can "daylight" onto an unobtrusive area of the lawn.

Pour a 6-inch layer of crushed stone or gravel into the bottom of the trench and lay a run of 4-inch perforated pipe (perforations down) along the entire length of the trench.

Next, fill the sides of the trench and cover the pipe with gravel. You can leave the surface exposed or fill it with soil and plant it. If you're planting, cover the gravel with landscape fabric to keep soil from washing into the rock. Tamp it and lay strips of sod.

CITY ORDINANCES

Local governments establish building codes to provide safety for residents and to ensure that construction is carried out with uniform standards. Once you finalize your plans, contact your local building department for the requirements that apply to your design. For example, you will find codes that specify how far fences and other structures must be set back from property lines. Many communities have rules that govern the height of fences and decks, the depth of utility lines and footings, as well as various materials and construction techniques that are acceptable and conform to safety standards. Local codes will probably require you to obtain building permits and schedule inspections.

CONCRETE FACTS

Concrete is a remarkably versatile material. In its liquid form it can be poured and formed into almost any shape, and when cured, it can support the weight of skyscrapers. It also lends itself to a variety of finishes—colored with premixed pigments, imbedded with decorative stone, or stamped with patterns that mimic brick.

Concrete is made from a mixture of portland cement, sand, gravel, and water. (Mortar, used for bonding brick and stone, contains lime instead of gravel.) The mixture is caustic, so wear gloves and durable clothing—and rubber boots if you'll be walking in it while pouring a large slab.

BUYING CONCRETE

You can purchase concrete in premixed bags or buy the ingredients separately and mix them on-site. Premix is more expensive but saves time and labor. Concrete for large driveway or patio slabs is better when purchased from a commercial ready mix company. Use the chart below to estimate the quantity you'll need, and remember that a cubic yard of concrete requires 40 to 50 bags of premix, depending on the weight.

Mixing concrete can be hard work, but small jobs such as setting fence posts or pouring small footings are well within the capabilities of most homeowners. Just buy the premix and add water.

Each project requiring concrete work will involve the same basic steps from start to finish. *(For more information on individual structures, see "Fences," pages 34–39, "Walls," pages 44–49, "Decks," pages 70–75, and "Patios," pages 76–81.)*

ESTIMATING QUANTITIES

Use this chart to estimate how much concrete you will need.

Cubic Yards of Concrete Needed
(1 cubic yard = 40 to 50 premixed bags)

Area (square feet)	Cubic yards needed for a:			
	3-inch slab	4-inch slab	5-inch slab	6-inch slab
10	.10	.14	.17	.20
25	.25	.34	.42	.51
50	.51	.68	.85	1.02
100	1.02	1.36	1.70	2.04

LAYING OUT THE SITE

Every project starts with measuring and laying out the area involved. For irregular shapes, use a rope or garden hose to define the perimeter so you can visualize it and make adjustments. Finalize the outline with spray paint. Outline straight edges precisely with mason's line stretched between stakes or batter boards. Dig holes for posts or footings to the depth required by local codes. Excavate for slabs to a depth needed for the concrete plus 6 inches for a gravel bed.

PREPARE THE BED

You'll need forms for slab work, but usually not for deck piers or footings—the excavation itself provides the form. Where forms are needed, use 2×4s for patio slabs, and taller forms for slabs that will support walls. Brace the forms where necessary and then install the gravel bed. Tamp it in place and lay wire reinforcing mesh supported on blocks so the mesh will be embedded in the center of the concrete. Now is the time to install conduit for electrical lines and pipe for plumbing.

ESTIMATE AND ORDER

For jobs that are less than ½ cubic yard, use premix or combine the ingredients in a wheelbarrow or mortar box. For up to a cubic yard, you can mix it yourself or use premix, depending on your budget, time, and experience. Any job requiring more than a cubic yard should be poured with ready mix, which usually is priced in ¼-yard increments beyond a base charge for small loads.

FROM MIX TO MASTERPIECE

Here are the steps you'll take for almost every concrete job.

PREMIX: Pour the bagged dry mix into a mortar box or wheelbarrow and use a hoe to make a depression in the center. Pour about two-thirds of the water required into the center of the hole and pull the ingredients together, first in one direction and then the other. Add the remaining water sparingly; the consistency you want will resemble a thick malt. Don't make it too thin.

DRY MIX: If you buy the ingredients separately, mix them in a formula of 1 part cement, 2 parts sand, and 3 parts gravel with ½ part water. Combine the dry ingredients thoroughly and then mix with water as you would for concrete from premixed bags.

POURING: Once your concrete is mixed, you'll have about two hours of working time before it begins to set up. Carry the mixed concrete in wheelbarrows and, after pouring, consolidate it by working a rod up and down in the mix. Spread the concrete with a garden rake and then pull a 2×4 across the forms to level the surface.

CURING: Concrete must be kept damp during the first week. You can keep moisture from evaporating by layering wet burlap bags or plastic sheets on its surface.

PORTABLE MIXERS

Rented concrete mixers are great time savers. They are available in capacities of ⅓ to 1 cubic yard. The size you will need depends on the scale of the project and how many helpers you can muster.

POURING FOOTINGS

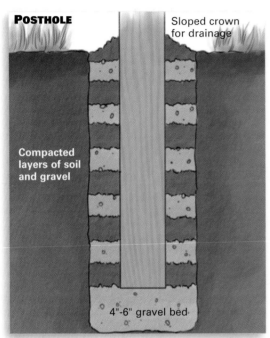

POSTHOLE

Sloped crown for drainage

Compacted layers of soil and gravel

4"-6" gravel bed

In some regions and for installations such as low decks, you may be able to anchor your posts in alternate layers of compacted soil and gravel. Check your building codes for footing requirements.

Wall footings should be as thick—and twice as wide—as the width of the wall. Advice on footings for specific projects is provided throughout this book. A footing should always rest on gravel.

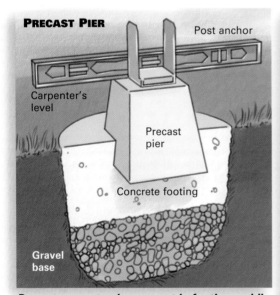

PRECAST PIER

Post anchor

Carpenter's level

Precast pier

Concrete footing

Gravel base

Precast concrete piers are set in footings while the concrete is still wet. Some have post anchors installed; others require a separate anchor. Footings and piers must be level.

CONCRETE FORM TUBE

Scrap wood frames

Form tube

Rebar

Prefabricated form tubes provide a convenient way to install poured footings. Hold them in place (about 8 inches above the bottom of the hole) with scrap wood frames.

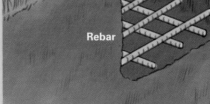

SELECTING LUMBER

Shop for lumber where you can inspect each board for problems such as cupping, warping, and excessive knots. Sight along the length of each board to be sure it isn't crooked or bowed. Straight lumber makes easier work and better results.

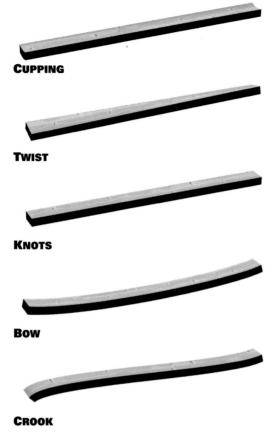

CUPPING

TWIST

KNOTS

BOW

CROOK

WASTE NOT, WANT NOT

This is an adage that does not apply to construction work. You'll waste a certain amount—it's unavoidable. Order 5 percent more than your materials list calls for.

LUMBER: WHAT SIZE IS IT REALLY?

After it is cut, lumber is dried, planed, and smoothed, which reduces its thickness and width. Nominal size (for example, "1×4") refers to the size before drying and planing; actual size means the size you actually get.

Nominal Size	Actual Size	Nominal Size	Actual Size
1×2	¾"×1½"	2×2	1½"×1½"
1×3	¾"×2¼"	2×4	1½"×3½"
1×4	¾"×3½"	2×6	1½"×5½"
1×6	¾"×5½"	2×8	1½"×7¼"
1×8	¾"×7¼"	2×10	1½"×9¼"
1×10	¾"×9¼"	2×12	1½"×11¼"
1×12	¾"×11¼"		

Wood is renewable, inexpensive, light, and durable. For landscaping, buy lumber that is treated or naturally resistant to rot, bugs, and weather.

Your supplier will stock two main types; leave the expensive hardwood to the indoor woodworkers and cabinetmakers. The category you want is called softwood, a term that indicates the kind of tree it comes from and not its strength.

LANDSCAPE FAVORITES

Redwood, cedar, and cypress—the best untreated species for outdoor projects— are attractive and extremely weather resistant. Douglas fir and southern pine are popular and less expensive.

REDWOOD: An excellent wood for exterior and interior projects, redwood has a close grain and is naturally resistant to weathering, warping, and cupping. There are more than 30 grades of redwood. A primary factor in redwood grading is appearance and color. Heartwood is reddish-brown; the outer layer or sapwood is cream-colored. Other grades are determined by the number and size of knots and the presence of stains or defects. Redwood is resistant to shrinkage. It is easy to cut and nail, and accepts wood finishes well.

CEDAR: Natural beauty and resistance to decay and insects characterize cedar. It is also easy to cut and nail and will uniformly accept wood finishes. Cedar is also graded by appearance and the number of knots, and is one of the "big three" woods for fences, decks, and gazebos.

CYPRESS: Native to wet or swampy areas of the South, cypress trees are naturally resistant to decay. Cypress is not as popular nationwide as redwood and cedar but is a favorite in the South, its native region.

Each of the above species is available in several grades, but only the heartwood of each is naturally resistant to weathering. Use heartwood for constant ground contact, such as posts or retaining walls. Use more economical construction grades above ground.

FIR AND PINE: These species are strong, lightweight, widely available, and less expensive than naturally resistant woods. They are available in two forms:

■ **Untreated lumber:** Commonly used for forms, batterboards, and disposable bracing, it won't hold up for long against the elements.

■ **Pressure-treated lumber:** A less expensive substitute for the durable redwood, cedar, and cypress, pressure-treated lumber—commonly fir or pine is extremely rot resistant. The chemicals forced into it under pressure make it resistant to weather and to insect attack. Usually chromated copper arsenate (CCA), the treatments are toxic, so wear impermeable gloves, long-sleeved shirts, and pants when handling the lumber. Wear a respirator when you saw it.

Treated lumber also comes in a variety of grades, from ground-contact rating for posts and retaining walls to lighter treatments for fences or deck boards. The durability depends on the amount of chemical treatment.

Other woods you may need, depending on the scope of your plans, are exterior grade plywood (for sheathing, subfloors, and walls) and T1-11 (a plywood siding that eliminates the need for sheathing).Your dealer can help you select the right wood for your project.

HOW FAR CAN JOISTS SPAN?

This table shows the lengths that can be spanned by various species when joists are set 16 inches on center.

SPECIES	GRADE	2×8	2×10	2×12
California Redwood	Sel. Struct.	12'-3"	15'-8"	19'-1"
	No. 1	12'-3"	15'-8"	19'-1"
	No. 2	11'-10"	15'-1"	18'-4"
Western Cedars	Sel. Struct.	11'-4"	14'-6"	17'-7"
	No.1	11'-4"	14'-6"	17'-7"
	No.2	11'-0"	14'-0"	17'-0"
Douglas Fir	Sel. Struct.	13'-4"	17'-0"	20'-9"
	No.1	13'-4"	17'-0"	20'-9"
	No.2	13'-1"	16'-9"	20'-4"
Southern Pine	Sel. Struct.	13'-1"	16'-9"	20'-4"
	No.1	13'-1"	16'-9"	20'-4"
	No.2	12'-10"	16'-5"	19'-11"

Note: Douglas fir and southern pine are common species that are pressure treated for resistance to rot and insects. Spans shown are for 40-pound live load—the standard required for residential floors.

GRADE STAMPS: WHAT THEY MEAN

All wood is stamped to provide information about the prevalence of defects, its species, grade, and moisture content. A grade stamp may also carry a number or the name of the mill that produced it and a certification symbol that shows the lumber association whose grading standards are used.

Pressure-treated lumber will carry a grade stamp that shows the year it was treated, the chemical used as a preservative, exposure condition (whether it can be used above ground or ground contact), and the amount of chemical treatment it received.

Plywood grading stamps also show whether the wood is suitable for ground contact or above-ground use, whether it can be used as sheathing, and numbers that indicate its thickness, and the distance it can span over rafters and joists. If the plywood will be exposed to weather, such as siding for a shed, look for a stamp reading EXTERIOR.

Many projects fail because the builder neglected to use lumber suited to a specific application. Be sure you use the grading stamps to help you choose lumber that will satisfy the strength requirements of your installation and withstand the vagaries of the weather.

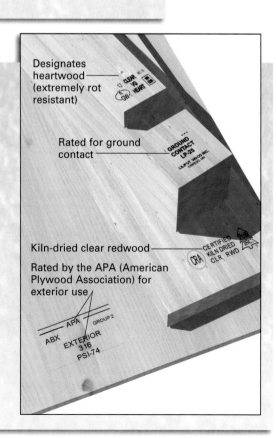

Designates heartwood (extremely rot resistant)

Rated for ground contact

Kiln-dried clear redwood

Rated by the APA (American Plywood Association) for exterior use

CARPENTRY: MEASURING AND CUTTING

USING SAWS

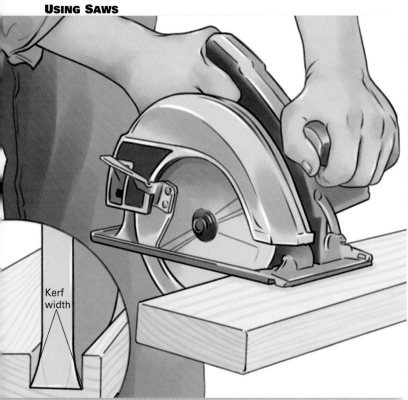

Use both hands to guide, not push, your circular saw. Always set the blade so that it penetrates no deeper than necessary. The width of the wood chewed into sawdust is called the blade's kerf.

Kerf width

To allow for the kerf, cut on the waste side of the mark (note the "X" at right).

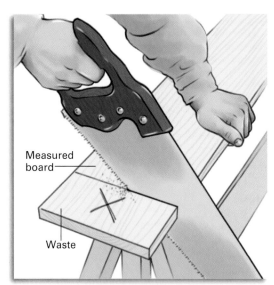

Measured board

Waste

WHICH SAW BLADES?

A crosscut blade is best for cutting across the wood grain (across the width of the board); a rip blade is best for cutting with the grain (parallel to the length of the board). Buy a quality combination blade for general use.

Measure twice and cut once. Follow that old carpenter's adage and you'll save time, wood, and frustration.

Precision isn't just for appearances; the strength of any structure depends on all framing members bearing precisely on each other at joints. Miscuts weaken structures.

MEASURING TOOLS

You won't need an abundance of tools for measuring. These few will get the job done:
TAPE: Get a 25-foot carpenter's rule with an inch-wide tape. Narrower tapes are flimsy; the inch-wide variety is handier for long dimensions, both vertical and horizontal.
COMBINATION SQUARE: Usually equipped with a level, a combination square lets you measure short dimensions quickly and mark lines for cutting at right angles.
FRAMING SQUARE: Bigger than a combination square, a framing square allows accurate measurement of large right angles.
LEVEL: For leveling and drawing straight edges. Purchase one that is 4 feet long.
CARPENTER'S PENCIL: Don't use desk pencils for marking lines. A carpenter's pencil has a thick lead that won't break as easily.

CUTTING TOOLS

These are the cutting tools you'll need:
CIRCULAR SAW: Your best friend on the job, it makes quick work of cutting chores.
HAND SAW: Use it to make precise cuts in thin stock.
SABER SAW: Often called a jig-saw, this versatile tool's specialty is cutting contours.
RECIPROCATING SAW: This sturdy tool tears into timbers and posts. It isn't essential, but it makes the work easier.
HACKSAW: Use this to chew through metal pipe and conduit.
HAND CHISELS: Get ½-inch and ¾-inch chisels and keep them sharp.
MITER BOX: Either hand or power models allow you to cut precise, matching angles.

WOODCUTTER'S TIPS

BE KERF CONSCIOUS: As a saw works, it chews its own width of wood into sawdust. The gap it leaves is called a kerf. If you measure and mark cuts with a pencil line, saw along the waste side of your line. If you cut on the wrong side of the pencil mark, you will remove wood from the piece you've measured, and your board will be that much shorter.
STAY SHARP: Dull tools make the work harder and more dangerous. Protect blades from damage. Repair or replace dull ones.

FASTENERS

When the fasteners in a structure fail, the whole thing begins to break down. Why jeopardize your whole project to save a few pennies per piece? Stick with quality fasteners.

WEATHER-RESISTANT

All hardware used for exterior projects should be stainless steel or labeled HDG for hot-dipped galvanized (dipped in zinc for rust resistance). Alternatives to galvanized nails include treated screws made for decks, fences, and other exterior structures.

GALVANIZED METAL CONNECTORS: Use galvanized metal connectors to fasten joints; they make stronger joints than toenailing and are made for a variety of installations:

■ **Joist hangers** nail to headers and form a saddle that supports the joists far more effectively than toenailing.

■ **Post/beam connectors** are designed for sturdy joints where posts fasten to a beam.

■ **Angle brackets** reinforce corners.

■ **Angle irons** attach stairs to concrete pads.

■ **Rafter tie-downs** secure roof rafters or trusses to the top of wall plates.

■ **Adjustable post bases** anchor the bottom of a post above concrete or wood and prevent water from rotting it.

■ **Deck post ties** secure rail posts to the deck structure.

■ **Staircase angles** secure steps to stair stringers without notching the stringers.

There are also connectors designed to eliminate face nailing through the boards. They eliminate exposed nails or screw heads on the top railing of a deck. For securing deck rails to posts from the underside, use deck railing ties; for securing deck boards to joists, use deck board ties.

COUNTERSUNK BOLTS

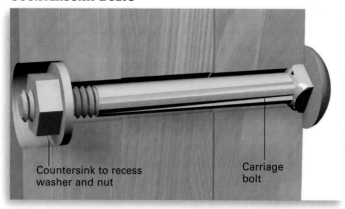

Countersink to recess washer and nut

Carriage bolt

If you don't like the look of bare galvanized hardware, you can mask it with spray paint—but choose a product that is specifically formulated for use on metal.

FASTENER TECHNIQUES

As you build wooden structures, keep these pointers in mind:

■ Screws and nails should be three times longer than the piece being anchored.

■ For more holding power, use common or box nails. Finishing nails are for trim only.

■ Do not drive finishing nails in all the way. Stop when the base of the head meets the surface of the trim. Then recess the nail with a nail set and cover it with wood putty.

■ When nailing a row of nails along the grain, avoid straight lines. Stagger the nails to avoid splitting the wood.

■ Drill pilot holes for lag screws.

■ Use beeswax to coat the threads of any screw that's hard to turn.

■ Use duplex nails (they have double heads) for temporary installations. The top head allows you to withdraw the nail for quick removal.

METAL CONNECTORS

To promote the use of forest products, the U.S. Department of Agriculture funded research on metal connectors for wood. That has led to the wide variety of metal connectors available at your home center. Metal connectors make a stronger wood joint than toenailing; the results can be seen in any hurricane area.

Rafters secured with metal tie-downs keep roofs from blowing away, while rafters that are nailed take flight. In addition to providing superior joint strength, metal connectors cradle the beam or joist in a joist hanger or post cap so you don't have to hold the workpiece while nailing.

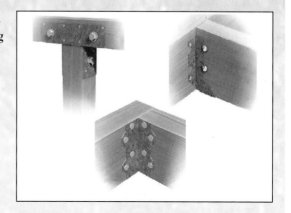

MASONRY

Brick and stone can bring a simple and long-lasting elegance to your landscape in a way that no other materials can. Before you start a masonry project, become familiar with the available materials and the techniques required.

BRICK BASICS

Brick is heavy, rough, labor-intensive, and so beautiful that you'll endure the hardship.
OPTIONS: Unlike wood, there are different types of brick for different uses, such as for walls, patios, fireplaces, and planters.
■ **COMMON BRICK** or building brick is used for walls and planters and is rated for its weather resistance: SW for severe-weather; MW for moderate climates; and NW for indoor use.
■ **PAVERS** are slightly larger than common brick and stand up to the hard treatment on patios and driveways.
■ **FIREBRICK** is yellow and, as the name implies, is used to line fireplaces and grills.
■ **FACE BRICK** has one side finished differently from another and is used where you need a finished appearance.
ESTIMATING AMOUNTS: Gauging the number of bricks for a wall is simple: six bricks to a square foot. For walls with two layers, double the amount. You can also easily estimate the number of bricks each course will require by dividing the length of the wall (in inches) by eight (the number of inches in a building brick). And the same waste rule applies to brick buying as to purchasing lumber—buy more than you estimate.

You can cut brick with a brickset or cold chisel, but if you lack experience and your project is a large one, rent a masonry saw. You'll reduce waste, and save time and money.

WORKING WITH STONE

Stonework can be an exciting challenge. It offers an outlet for artistic flair but requires a good deal of patience in finding just the right type of stone, and in cutting and laying it.

Stone is available in the following forms:
NATURAL FLAGSTONE is flat and has irregular shapes and thicknesses. You can also buy precut squares with uniform thickness.
FIELD STONE also comes in irregular shapes but is usually round and its size varies (sometimes greatly).
ASHLAR STONE is uniformly thick (for stacking), but the lengths of the pieces vary.

You can also buy manufactured stone—man-made concrete castings with interlocking lips (a foolproof feature that makes this product a good do-it-yourself choice).

Flagstone and brick can be laid over a sand base, and natural or manufactured stone can simply be stacked to form a decorative wall. Brick or stone and sand—dry-laid masonry—is a good choice for a cold climate because structures will not crack from frost heave as ones with wet-laid masonry slabs can. Cut stone with the same techniques used to cut brick, but waste is not as much of an issue. You can usually find space for the leftovers.

MORTARING

Mortar does not contain gravel, but usually does contain lime, which makes it easier to work and smooth. You can buy the mortar mix (1 part mason's cement and 3 parts sand) in 60- or 80-pound bags. Just add water a little at a time. Or make your own: 1 sack (94 pounds) portland cement, 6 cubic feet of damp sand, and 50 pounds of hydrated lime. Mix the mortar for small projects in a mortar box. When the mix sticks to an upside-down trowel, it's ready to use.

If you build masonry walls with mortar, you must pour a concrete footing for the project. Without a footing, the heaving of frozen earth will crack the mortar.

Stone and brick make effective retaining walls and can be used to define spaces and separate one area from another.

ELECTRICAL WIRING

Local building codes vary in their requirements for electrical work. In some communities, all major electrical installations must be done by a licensed electrician. In others, homeowners can do it themselves. But in all cases, major electrical work requires permits and inspections. Check with your local building department before proceeding.

GFCI OUTLETS

Outdoor circuits must plug into special outlets called Ground Fault Circuit Interrupters (often labeled GFI or GFCI). These outlets are designed to sense a short in the line (caused, for example, by a person coming into contact with a live circuit) and immediately cut the power. GFCIs are required by law on some indoor receptacles and on all outdoor receptacles.

LOW VOLTAGE

One electrical project that can be completed easily by an enterprising homeowner is low-voltage outdoor lighting. Such systems use a transformer to step down house current to a much safer 12 volts. Most systems are available in kits with complete instructions. To install low-voltage wiring, cut a wire trench in the turf, lay the cable in the trench, and connect each fixture to the cable with a clamp connector. The cable will terminate at a lamp on one end and a transformer on the other. Most transformers are designed to mount to a hard surface and plug—with a short cord—into a GFCI outlet.

NEW CIRCUITS

If you are adding outdoor electrical circuits, it's best to install new circuit wiring at the service panel so the outdoor wiring is separate from the rest. Complete the outdoor wiring before you connect it to the service panel to prevent any danger of electrical shock while you work on the circuits.

If you install a lighting circuit, install a 15-amp breaker and use 14-2W\G wire. This designation means the wire is 14 gauge (a measure of its thickness and load capacity), and has two main wires with a third for grounding. If the circuit will be used for appliances or tools, install a 20-amp breaker and use heavier 12-2W\G wire.

If the wires will be exposed—not fully enclosed in a wall or underground—run them in steel conduit to protect them from damage. If the wiring will be underground, use steel conduit buried at least six inches deep; or use

INSTALLING OUTDOOR RECEPTACLES

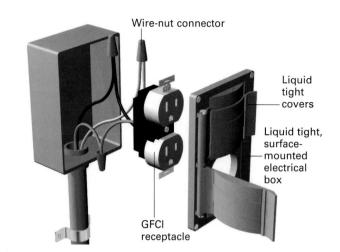

Wire-nut connector

Liquid tight covers

Liquid tight, surface-mounted electrical box

GFCI receptacle

plastic conduit buried at least 18 inches deep. Wiring left above ground must be encased in steel conduit.

Always use full lengths of wire between receptacles. Electrical codes prohibit splices between the ends of a circuit. Splices are permitted only at junction boxes.

All conduit, connectors, electrical boxes, and covers must be made specifically for outdoor use and must be liquid tight to prevent water from entering the system and causing electrical shorts or shock.

SAFE CONNECTIONS

To make a safe and professional-looking wire connection at receptacles, first strip the insulation back about 2 inches from the ends of the wires. Hold the wire so the insulation is snug against the wire screw of the receptacle. Wrap the wire around the wire screw in a clockwise direction, then tighten the screw. Now cut the wire with a wire cutters (use a tool called a diagonal cutters) next to the wire screw, leaving a tight, tailless connection.

Remember that you must have the electrical wiring inspected before you close up trenches or cover over the electrical outlets so the inspector has a full view of the work.

PRECAUTIONS

Because of the potential hazard that electrical work poses, always remember to:
■ Make sure the power is turned off to the circuit you are working on.
■ Never run a circuit at more than 80 percent of its power rating in amps.
■ Have all work inspected before it is covered with earth or by wall surfaces.

DEFINING SPACE:
FENCES & WALLS

A garden wall of used brick is rustic and inexpensive. Shop for used brick at salvage yards. The flowers add color and soften the stark effect of a plain wall.

Wonderfully versatile, fences and walls do far more than mark property lines. They corral pets and keep out strays, frame things you want to showcase and hide things you don't want to see. They can lift vines to new heights and knock down high winds. Fences define spaces, separating one from another. Walls impart a sense of permanence to the landscape, blocking erosion of the soil and standing firm against future whims of design. Time only enhances their beauty and your reputation for having had the foresight to build them well.

PROPERTY BOUNDARIES: WHERE TO DRAW THE LINE

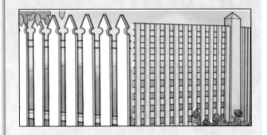

Before you build a fence or wall on the edge of your property, know where the edge is. A plot map of your land (available at your local courthouse) will help, but you can be certain only with markers on the property itself. Use a metal detector to check for stakes marking the corners. If they're not there, get a survey to prevent boundary disputes and avoid questions that would arise when you sell your home.

A fence can define property boundaries and provide security. The traditional picket fence is an easy do-it-yourself project; you can also buy pre-cut pickets.

Arborvitae frame this white lattice privacy fence. A pathway in the garden leads to a bench where you can relax as you contemplate nature's (and your own) handiwork.

Low-level foliage provides color and eliminates grass or weed-trimming between this brick path and the wooden privacy fence.

This concrete retaining wall controls erosion and diverts water runoff from the hill behind. A concrete wall can be stuccoed in the color of your choice.

A traditional New England-style stone fence is popular where stones are readily available. The stones can be laid loose or mortared.

FENCE POSTS

Determine the fence post spacing, then attach mason's lines to the batter boards to lay out the fence line. Position and brace the corner posts. String a line between the tops of the corner posts and use it to align the line posts.

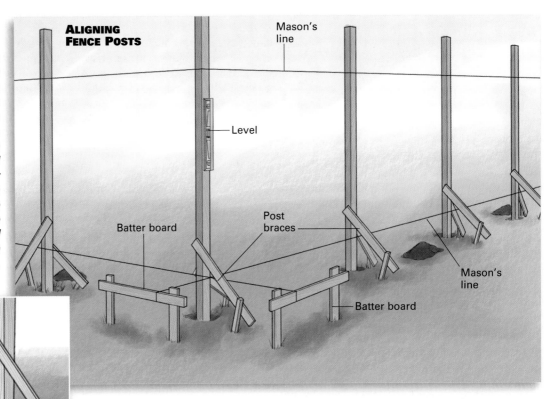

ALIGNING FENCE POSTS

Mason's line

Level

Batter board

Post braces

Mason's line

Batter board

To hold the post plumb, set braces on adjacent faces of the post. Use a 2-pound hammer to drive them into the soil and a cordless drill and temporary screws to attach them to the posts.

No matter what kind of fence you want, establish a precise layout before you build. Before putting a fence near a property line, check local codes for any setback requirements that might restrict how close you can build to the edge of your land.

LAYING OUT CORNERS

Drive temporary stakes at the locations you've chosen for your corner or end posts. Now build batter boards—two pointed 2×4 legs with a crossbar at least 2 feet long. Batter boards give you something sturdy on which to tie your cord, and you can adjust your alignment at the crossbar. Drive the batter boards into the ground at each end, with two at the corners as shown *above.*

THE RIGHT STRING: Tie a mason's line to a nail in one crossbar (don't use household string, which stretches and sags). Cinch it up tight to the batter board at the opposite end.

THE RIGHT ANGLE: To make sure a corner is square, measure 3 feet from the corner along one line and mark it with tape. On the other line, mark a spot 4 feet from the corner. Now measure between the marks. If the distance is 5 feet, congratulations—your corner is square. If not, adjust the lines until your diagonal distance is exactly right.

SPACING

When your corner-, end-, and gate-post locations are marked, determine the spacing you'll use between the line posts. No single distance is best for all circumstances, but 8 feet is probably the most common.

CUSTOM: If you design the fence, you get to set the rules. But keep these facts in mind:
■ Posts set farther apart require less work and fewer posts, but the fence isn't as strong.
■ Heavy fences need more support; that requires sturdier posts set closer together.
■ For board fencing, space posts in even multiples of feet; that's how the fence boards are sold. Odd-measure spacing requires extra sawing and wastes material.

CHAIN LINK: If you're installing chain link, space posts 6 or 8 feet apart.

PANELS: For prefabricated wood fence panels, set up the panels temporarily as you go and set stakes at the end of each panel.

When you know where the posts will go, mark their locations with stakes.

DEPTH

How deep do you dig the postholes? As a rule of thumb, posthole depth should be one-half the exposed height of the post (3 feet deep for a 6-foot fence) or at least 6 inches below the

WOOD OR METAL FENCE?

Your choice of materials will depend on your fencing objective (beauty, security or windbreak, for example), the design of your landscape, and your budget.

■ Chain link, a suburban standard, is inexpensive and easy to install. It marks boundaries and offers some security. You can improve its all-too-functional appearance with vinyl coating, paint, or climbing vines.

■ Wrought-iron fences—long popular in the East and South—complement Victorian and early American styles. Wrought iron is more expensive and its installation is more demanding than chain link or wood. But it can be custom-made to fit the style of your landscape. A wrought-iron fence with a sturdy gate and pointed post caps can discourage intruders.

■ Wood, perhaps the most economical fencing, is certainly the most versatile, from a ranch, split-rail style to cottage-cute pickets.

■ Privacy fences can be constructed board-on-board, board-and-trellis, trellis, post-and-rail, solid board, or woven wood, depending on your taste. Add built-in seating and a shady overhead—or windows—to create "view fencing."

frost line if your soil freezes in the winter. Your local building department or weather service can tell you what the maximum frost depth is in your area. Add 4 inches to this depth because you will be putting in a gravel base for drainage.

DIGGING HOLES

Use a posthole digger (see "Make Your Digging Easy," below) to dig each hole at the location marked. No matter what tool you use, wear gloves—this is blistering work. Even with power tools, your shoulders and back will get a workout, so allow plenty of time.

SOAK IT: If you run into clay or hard soil, pour water in the hole. Move on to the next hole while the water settles. Then come back to dig out the softened mud.

SHARP IDEA: Keep a sharp spade, an ice-scraper, or other long blade handy for slicing through tree roots.

SETTING POSTS

Shovel 4 inches of gravel into each end and corner posthole and tamp the gravel with a 2×4. Using your mason's line, set the posts in each hole and make sure they're plumb. Level all sides of each post. If you're building a wooden fence, plumb them with a level and brace them until you've poured the concrete.

Fill the corner and end postholes with concrete, rechecking them for plumb. Run a steel rod or 2×4 up and down in the concrete to release trapped air.

Overfill the holes so the concrete mounds up about 2 inches above ground. Slope it away from the posts to allow for water runoff. Set line posts in the same way, bracing, plumbing, and filling with concrete. Then let the concrete cure three to seven days before installing the rest of the fence.

In some regions, you can use compacted soil and gravel. Check with your local building department for requirements.

Using a shovel, fill the hole with concrete. Slope the surface with a trowel to allow water runoff.

MAKE YOUR DIGGING EASY

There are three types of posthole diggers that make short work of digging holes. Mark the desired hole depth on the side of your tool. When the mark reaches ground level, quit digging.

■ A clamshell digger has two handles and two blades. Drive the digger into the ground, spread the handles to grip the soil, then lift and empty. These work best in shallow holes.

■ A manual auger has a round blade that screws into the ground as you turn it. It works best in loose soil.

■ A gas-powered auger churns into even compacted soil. Digging is still hard work because the auger is cumbersome; most require two operators. They're rented on a daily rate, so you can save cost and strain by lining up friends to get the holes dug in a day.

BUILDING AND INSTALLING A FENCE

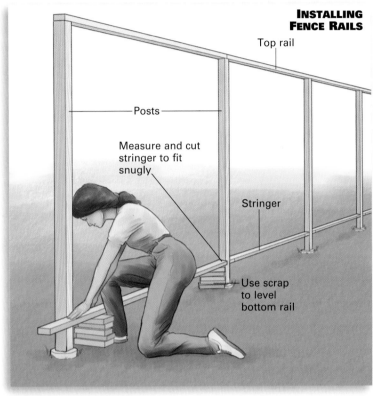

INSTALLING FENCE RAILS

Top rail

Posts

Measure and cut stringer to fit snugly

Stringer

Use scrap to level bottom rail

RAIL JOINT OVER POST

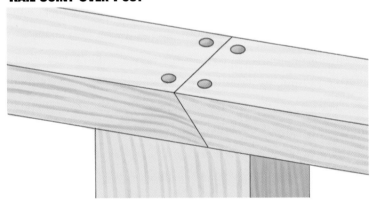

RAIL NAILING INTERVAL

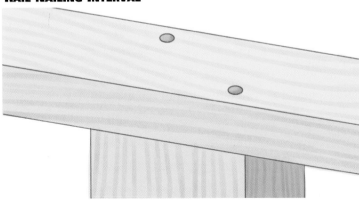

Outdoor landscape projects just don't get any more straightforward than fencing. Once you've set the posts, you build a framework, add the rails, panels, or other surface, then stand back and marvel at the change in your yard's personality.

WOODEN FRAMES

After the concrete around your posts has set, mark the tops of the posts for cutting. The method depends on your terrain:

■ **Level ground:** Run mason's line at the fence height from one corner post to another, using a line level to keep things straight.

■ **Hillside sites:** You can choose to make a stepped, sloped, or sloped-with-a-stepped framework (*see "Fencing on a Slope," opposite*).

When the posts are marked and you've checked the height twice, a reciprocating saw is the best tool for lopping the tops off smoothly and straight.

TOP RAILS: Next, measure and cut the top rail pieces. Because the top rail serves as both a nailer for fence panels and adds strength to the structure, use the longest pieces of top rail possible, butting them over the center of the posts where a new piece begins. Use the rectangular and diagonal nailing patterns (*shown bottom left*); predrill the ends of the top rail before nailing.

STRINGERS: Measure and cut 2×4 stringers to fit snugly between the posts. You can toenail these joints, but metal rail hangers will make a stronger joint. Position the stringers about 6 inches above ground.

PANELS: To avoid water damage, install panels 2 or more inches above ground. If you want to enclose the space between the boards and the ground, install a replaceable kickboard (*below*).

SKIRT BOARD BELOW BOTTOM RAIL

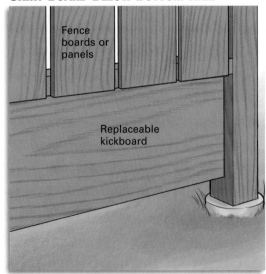

Fence boards or panels

Replaceable kickboard

FENCING ON A SLOPE

Sloped fencing requires a different method for laying out line posts. Be sure to note the differences.

STEPPED FENCE

To lay out line posts for stepped fencing, set end posts in concrete and run mason's line from the top of the lower post to the base of the upper post. On the line, mark the intermediate post locations with tape, drop a plumb bob at each mark, and drive a stake. Set the intermediate posts and use the mason's line to mark their tops for cutting. Dig postholes and set the line posts in concrete.

Install the top rails and stringers so they are level, using rail hangers where the rails join the posts. Install the fence boards perpendicular to the top rails *(shown right)* or, as an alternative, parallel to the rails and stringers. If you prefer to enclose the space between the bottom stringers and the ground, cut kickboards and nail or screw them to the bottom stringers.

SLOPED FENCE

To set the line posts for a sloped fence, set corner posts in concrete and run a chalk line from the lower to the upper post (at fence height on both ends). Mark post locations with a plumb bob as you would for a stepped fence. Keep the line in place until the posts are set and snap it to mark the cutting angle. Cut the posts with a reciprocating saw.

Cut the top rail and stringers at an angle and install them so they fit snugly between the posts

Cut the bottom ends of the fence boards at the required angle, mount them, and cut the tops to a chalked line. Or, using a template made from a 1×4, you can cut the tops of each panel piece separately and install them parallel to the posts.

SLOPED WITH A STEPPED FRAMEWORK

This method combines stepped and sloped fencing. Set the line posts and install the top rail and stringers as you would on a sloped fence. Using narrow stock, cut the points on the fence boards and temporarily nail a 2×4 to the posts. This guide should match the angle of the slope and should be placed where the bottoms of the panels will terminate. Set each fence board on the 2×4 and screw it to the top rail and stringer. When you have finished fastening the fence boards, remove the temporary guide.

To build a more rigid fence, install fence framing as shown in the inset illustration. Cut the top rails and stringers at an angle matching the slope of the ground. Then install intermediate level stringers to brace the top rails and bottom stringers. Cut the intermediate stringer ends at an angle so they fit tightly against the members they support.

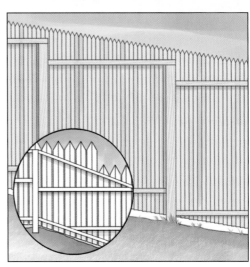

BUILDING AND INSTALLING A FENCE
continued

Vary the fence height to meet different needs. The panels on this patio offer privacy and safety. Those at the rear of the yard define the property lines without blocking the view.

Lattice screens provide privacy while letting air and sunshine filter through. They are difficult to stain or seal after construction, so stain or seal all surfaces before assembly.

LATTICE PANEL FENCING

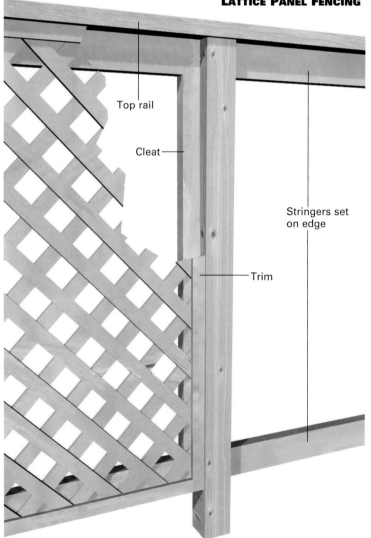

Top rail

Cleat

Stringers set on edge

Trim

PRIVACY SCREENS

Privacy screens will set areas in your yard apart and let the breeze come through. They can be built with lattice or boards set louver-style—either vertically or horizontally. Louvered privacy screens also make excellent windbreaks if you overlap the edges.

Construction starts with the same framework as any wooden fencing; 4×4 posts are plumbed, braced, and set in concrete (*see "Aligning Fence Posts" on page 34*).

CONSTRUCTION: You can be a little daring with the top rail; instead of a plain 2×4, use a 2×6 with edges cut in a decorative pattern.

You won't need a top stringer on a louvered fence, just one on the bottom. A lattice needs top and bottom stringers set on edge. Center the stringers (in metal rail connectors) flush between the posts. Then nail 1×2 cleats inside the posts as nailers for the vertical edges of the screen. Align the cleats with the top and bottom stringers. For horizontal louvers, cut cleats and attach them at an angle to the posts. For vertical louvers, attach the cleats to the top rail and bottom stringer.

PROTECTION: To provide moisture protection, apply a coat of clear wood sealer or stain to both the frame and lattice before assembling them. Then cut the lattice panels to fit and nail them to the stringers and the cleats. Finish off your panels with quarter-round or 1×2 trim at their edges.

Using another method, you can cut grooves in the center of the top rail, bottom stringer, and posts, and insert the lattice pieces into the grooves instead of nailing them in place.

CHAIN-LINK FENCE

Although galvanized steel is the most common—and the most durable—material for chain-link fencing, aluminum is also available. The mesh (or "fabric") is sold in 4-, 5-, and 6-foot heights. Include a 2-inch ground clearance when setting the height of your fence.

COMPLETE KIT: Posts and rails provide the basic framework, and the fabric is attached to them with hardware—top rail, end caps, tension bars, and tension bands (the bands clamp around the posts and hold the tension bars in them). Your distributor will supply the complete package of materials.

Set posts (see "Aligning Fence Posts" on page 34) at intervals that divide one run into equal lengths, usually 6 to 8 feet. Make sure the exposed height of the post is high enough for your mesh (add 2 inches for line posts and 3 inches for the heftier corner and end posts).

ATTACHING HARDWARE:
Attach three tension bands to each corner and end post, install hinges and latches to gate posts, and end caps to corner and end posts. Leave all hardware loosely in position for now; you'll tighten it when everything is in place.

Put line post (or loop) caps on each line post and slide the top rail through them. Splice joints with a connector and cut the rail to proper lengths with a hacksaw. Fit the top rail into the end caps and adjust them to their desired height. Drive a post cap onto each corner and end post.

INSTALLING FABRIC: Starting at one corner, unroll the mesh on the ground.

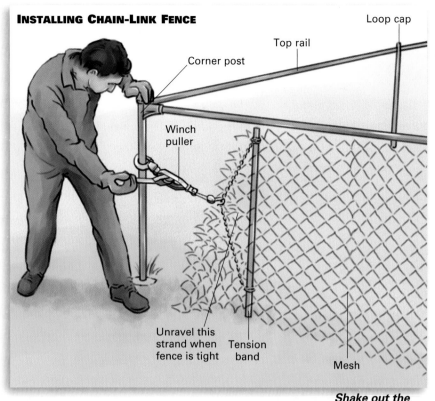

INSTALLING CHAIN-LINK FENCE

Loop cap
Top rail
Corner post
Winch puller
Unravel this strand when fence is tight
Tension band
Mesh

Thread a tension bar through one end. Next, attach the tension bar to the tension bands. Tie the mesh loosely to the top rail.

Push a tension bar through the fabric about 3 feet from the other end or corner post. Attach a puller (a winch pulley) to the bar and pull the fabric until you can compress the loops about ¼ inch. Keeping the tension on, insert another tension bar in the mesh, and unravel one strand of fabric at the end (use pliers). Attach the bar to the tension bands.

FINISHING UP: Make any adjustments to the height and tighten everything down. Tie the fabric to the rails and line posts with wire.

Shake out the mesh and use wire ties to attach it loosely to the top rail. Use a winch puller or cable jack (available at rental outlets) attached to an end post to stretch the mesh to the opposite end or corner.

FENCING ALTERNATIVES

Wrought iron fencing has a rich appeal and its panels can be custom-made. It requires metal-working and welding skills, so a contractor may have to install it.

Aluminum fencing can be customized to fit many different styles, and can be a maintenance-free, look-alike alternative to wrought iron. Because aluminum fence components are assembled with stainless steel screws and epoxy adhesives, it can be installed by the homeowner.

Do-it-yourselfers like vinyl fencing material because most components snap together without fasteners or tools. It is maintenance free and relatively inexpensive. See the yellow pages for a list of fence dealers in your area.

Painting can provide contrasts—here, to the brick wall. The lightweight pickets reduce the weight of the gate, minimizing the potential for sags and undue wear on the hinges.

GATES

Gates are outdoor doorways. They say "welcome" to friends and neighbors and are as important to your overall design as any other landscape element.

THE RIGHT WIDTH

The right width for your gate depends on what you'll take through it. If it's just people, 32 inches is wide enough. Mowers and wheelbarrows? Now you're looking at a 42-inch gate for comfortable elbow room. Vehicles need a gate at least 10 feet wide.

Measure some gates around your neighborhood. Then measure your yard equipment. Remember that you won't always have the wheelbarrow aimed perfectly straight, and hinges and latches may get in the way, so don't cut your width too close.

MATERIALS

Gates are subject to frequent slamming and vibration. To keep them from sagging or falling apart, use materials that make the gate attractive and durable.

POSTS: Apply clear wood sealer to redwood or cedar posts, or use pressure-treated wood. Make your gate posts oversized—4×4s for line posts, 6×6s for gate or corner posts. Add an inch more than the gate width to the space between the posts to leave room for the hinges and to keep the gate from binding.

WEIGHT: To reduce gate weight, use smaller framing members—2×3s rather than 2×4s—and lightweight redwood rather than treated lumber. Any gate over 4 feet wide weighs heavily on the hinges. So if you are building a 10-foot-wide gateway for your driveway, use two 5-foot gates that latch at the center.

JOINTS: Gate joints should never be butted and toenailed. If your design permits, use half-lap or rabbet-and-gusset with dowel-and-glue construction for these joints (*see illustration, page 41*). For added strength, use screws and exterior waterproof resorcinol glue.

HARDWARE: Use weather-resistant screws—not nails—for gate construction, predrilling first. Screws have better holding power than nails, and you need all the strength you can get in a gate. All gate hardware should be nickel- or chrome-plated, or galvanized.

Do not use butt hinges for a gate. They are too small to support its weight. Buy the largest and strongest strap and gate hinges that are compatible with the size and style of your gate.

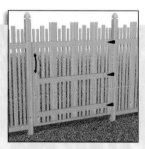

MATERIALS

In most cases, the selection of gate materials is based on the choice of fencing. Climate, durability, maintenance, and design can also affect your choices.

Wood is durable, requires moderate maintenance, and provides the opportunity to create your own design.

Wrought iron can rust and must be painted periodically in humid climates.

Aluminum gates are assembled with stainless steel fasteners, making aluminum a good choice for pool enclosures.

Galvanized steel will rust in time; choose vinyl-coated chain link for long-term weather resistance.

Vinyl sets light-duty boundaries or can accent a garden—and it won't rust. Vinyl fences are not secure, however.

GATE CONSTRUCTION

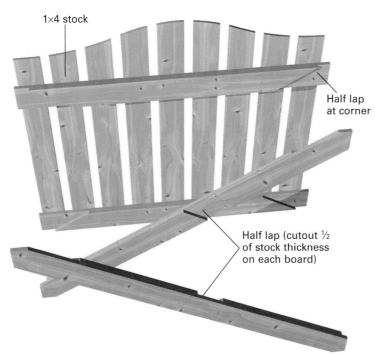

1×4 stock

Half lap
at corner

Half lap (cutout ½
of stock thickness
on each board)

*For gate strength, use half-lap rather than butt joints. You remove
half the wood on the two joining members to make half-lap joints.
Use a dado blade in your table or radial-arm saw to make the
joints. Also, use treated screws and resorcinol glue at all joints.*

GATE CORNER CONSTRUCTION

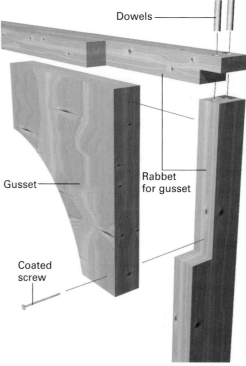

Dowels

Gusset

Rabbet
for gusset

Coated
screw

*If your gate design does not include a brace, use
rabbet joints with reinforcing plywood gussets at
the four corners of the frame. The gussets
strengthen the joints and add a nice design detail.*

BUILDING A WOODEN GATE

You can build a wooden gate to match your
fence design, or customize the design so the
gate accents your entryway.
START WITH Z: Measure the gate opening
at both the top and bottom (the
measurements may be slightly different).
To build a simple box frame with a Z-brace,
(you won't need fancy joints) cut 2×4s for the
top and bottom, one inch less (for clearance)
than your gate-space measurements. Attach
the 2×4 sides.

Lay the diagonal support piece under
opposite corners of the frame and mark the
angle formed by the corners. Cut and screw
the support in place. Then test-fit the frame.
ALIGN HINGES: Once you're sure
everything will fit correctly, mount the fence
boards, lattice, or decorative panels, drilling
all holes before screwing them on the frame.
Screw or bolt the hinges to the gate,
positioning the hinges so they are on center
at about ¼-inch outside the gate. Make sure
they are vertical and in line with each other.

Place wood blocks under the gate to hold
it at the desired level (high enough to clear
the ground when the gate is opened).

Center the gate in the opening,
mark the hole locations on the post,
predrill, and mount the gate with
one or two screws in each hinge.
NON-BINDING: Does the gate
swing freely? If it binds along the
latch edge, use a sander to round
over the latch edges lightly. Install
the remaining screws and the latch.

CHAIN-LINK GATES

Gates for chain-link fences are sold
as prefab units and include hinges,
latches, and hardware. They nearly
hang themselves. Dealers supply
slightly larger posts to support the
gate, so installation of a chain link
gate is a relatively simple project.

GATE HINGES

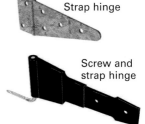

Strap hinge

Screw and
strap hinge

*Choose hinges that are
designed specifically for
gates, such as the gate
hinges shown here. The
lower hinge is attached to
the post with a 4-inch lag
hook that penetrates deep
into the wood.*

HINGES

Your choice of hinges can be critical to the success of your gate.
Remember that the hinges alone support the gate, so hinge quality
is most important. For durability, always use hinges that are
nickel-plated or galvanized.

WALL BASICS

Landscape construction can be artistic as well as utilitarian. This treatment of forms, planes, and textures required only basic skills but uncommon vision.

Good walls, well made, add style and a sense of permanence to a landscape. When you need to define space, create privacy, or hold back a slope, a wall does the job with style.

Before you begin, check local building codes for limits on wall height and setback.

MATERIALS

CONCRETE BLOCK has strength and economy in its favor. Its functional appearance may limit where you use it. **BRICK** has great versatility in its many surface finishes and patterns. Affordable **TIMBER** has a rustic quality that complements many landscapes. So does **STONE,** but it's fairly costly unless you have a private source and a way to haul it. **PRECAST DECORATIVE STONES,** either pinned (with holes for inserting rebar) or interlocking, are self aligning and take the guesswork out of positioning. They are especially useful if you need to build a retaining wall.

Consider the materials already present in your landscape, and the impact your new wall will have on the overall design. Choose materials that reflect the natural look of your region and the architectural style of your neighborhood, your house, and other landscape structures near it.

If the choices get to be overwhelming, take pictures of your site to a gardening center or a professional landscaper. They can help you narrow the alternatives.

As you consider the design features of materials, evaluate the amount of work each requires and strike a balance between design, budget and your skills. Stacked landscaping timbers make wall-building easy. So do dry-stacked walls—easy, but heavy. Mortaring brick and stone requires some special skills, so you may not want to tackle it yourself or without experienced help.

WORK CREW

Building a wall requires lots of lugging and lifting, so it's wise—and more fun—to have some volunteer help, at least two strong workers (more, if possible). If your friends have some experience and construction skills, so much the better. You'll discover that friends with the most building savvy will have fewer prior commitments if you mention the "builder's buffet" you'll be serving on the worksite. (A pizza fulfills your obligation.)

LAYING OUT A WALL

The technique for laying out a wall is much the same as laying out a fence (*see "Aligning Fence Posts" on page 34*). First, make batter boards from 2×4s and drive them into the ground about 1½ feet beyond the wall corners. Stretch mason's lines between the crosspieces of the batter boards. The strings should outline your wall, intersecting over the corners.

Brick

Precast (pinned)

Precast (border)

BUILDING A TIMBER WALL

To assemble a wood retaining wall, use barn spikes or predrill aligned holes through timbers and install steel rebar to join the timbers.

SQUARE? Corners must be precise. Here's how to check for square: Measure along two strings from the corner where they intersect— mark a point four feet from the corner along one string, and a point three feet from the corner along the other string. Adjust the lines until the marks are five feet apart. Then the corner is square. Tweak your mason's lines until all corners pass this test.

With the strings squared up, drop a plumb line at each corner and and mark it with a stake. Then stretch a line at the base of the stakes and use chalk or spray paint to mark the course (a single layer of stone). Leave the line and batter boards in place: you'll need them to line up the courses.

FIRM FOOTING

Walls need better support than they can get from bare ground. Your choice of a gravel bed or concrete footings depends on the type of wall you build.

DRY-STACKED WALL: You won't need footings for a wall that is set without mortar, or "dry-stacked." Footings keep walls from cracking with frost heave, and since there is no mortar in a dry-stacked wall, there's nothing to crack. The pieces shift and settle with the frost. Dry-stacked walls do need a bed, however—a trench about 8 inches deep, as wide as the wall, with 6 inches of tamped gravel for drainage. And all stone retaining walls require a drainage trench to keep water from backing up behind them (*see "Water Disposal" in the next column*).

MORTARED WALLS: Mortared walls require footings twice as wide as the wall and deep enough to extend below the frost line.

Frost depth varies by region and soil type. In one area, for instance, sandy well-drained soil may freeze to a depth of perhaps a foot, while just miles away clay soil may be frozen to a depth of 4 feet. Check with your local building department to find the frost depth for your area.

■ **FORMS:** Build them with 2×8s and tie them together with 1× scrap across the top to keep the weight of the concrete from bowing them. Make sure the inside dimensions—not the outside—conform to the footing width required. Once your forms are set and leveled, lay in rebar for reinforcement—two horizontal (parallel to the edges) and vertical lengths at intervals that are appropriate for your materials.

RETAINING WALLS

Retaining walls must hold back the pressure of the earth and water behind them, so they must be designed with special considerations.

WATER DISPOSAL: If you are building a solid retaining wall on a sloped site, water running down the slope and the back side of the wall surface must not be permitted to build up behind it. When you excavate for a retaining wall, dig the trench wide enough for the first course plus an extra foot into the slope. Lay one or two courses. Then pour a 4-inch gravel drainage bed, sloping it 1 inch for every 4 feet. Lay 4-inch perforated drainpipe and 4 more inches of gravel. Cover it with landscape fabric and then with soil and sod. The drainpipe must end at a storm drain or a catch basin.

To maintain a uniform slope on the face of a stone wall, cut a scrap of plywood diagonally so it is 2 inches wider for every foot of length. Use a level to plumb the panel's straight side.

When laying a stone wall, sort the stones into separate piles by size and shape. Use the largest stones in the lower courses, long stones perpendicular to the wall to tie the front and rear together.

If your wall is dry-stacked stone or timber, the spaces between the materials will act as "weep holes" and let the water pass through. You can also drill 1-inch holes every 2 feet in the second course of a timber wall to improve drainage. Landscape fabric behind the wall will keep soil from washing through.

STAGGERED COURSES: When laying timber or stone retaining walls, each succeeding course must be staggered backward into the slope. Staggering adds strength and will keep the wall from bowing over time. To stagger the face, set the front edge of each succeeding course about an inch back from the preceding one.

BUILDING TIPS (SO YOUR WALL WON'T)

When building *a timber retaining wall*, use only timbers that are treated for ground contact. They are slightly more expensive than lightly-treated timbers, but the cheaper timbers will rot and the wall will fail earlier.

For *dry-laid rock walls*, use sedimentary flat stones such as ashlar and flagstone. Lay the thickest and largest stones for the first course. Set the longest stones perpendicular to the wall as bond stones to tie the wall together.

When *using fieldstone*, sort by size. Use the largest stones for the first course, and use the small stones as fillers, spaced uniformly throughout the wall.

MORTARED STONE WALLS

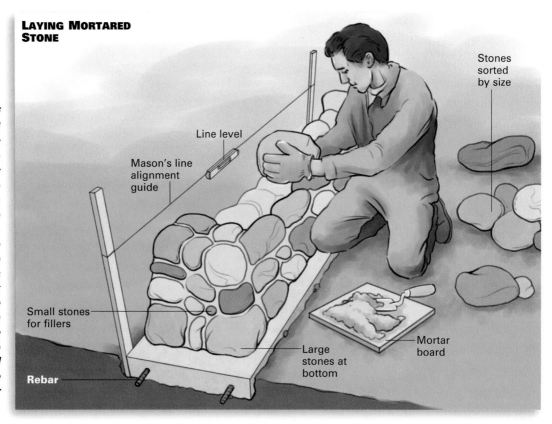

LAYING MORTARED STONE

Stones sorted by size

Line level

Mason's line alignment guide

Small stones for fillers

Rebar

Large stones at bottom

Mortar board

Laying stones of irregular size will result in mortar joints that are not uniform or straight. Use mason's line as a guide to keep the wall plumb. At its base, the mortar bed atop the footings must be thick enough to fill the joints between stones. Use small stones to fill gaps and reduce the size of the mortar joints.

"Like a rock." From poets to truckmakers, people have turned to stone as the standard—the symbol of durability. Styles come and go, but stone stays. And with mortar, it also stays put. If that's what you want in a landscape wall, here's how to get it.

LAYOUT

Review "Laying out a Wall" (*page 42*). Make batter boards from 2×4s and drive them into the ground 1½ feet beyond the points you've selected for the ends and corners of your wall. Run mason's line between the batter boards to define the wall's edge.

TEST SQUARE: So the corners *look* square? Be sure. From an intersection of your mason's lines, measure 3 feet along one line and mark it. From the same intersection, measure 4 feet along the other line. Adjust the lines on the batter boards until the diagonal measurement between your marks is exactly 5 feet.

Drop a plumb line at each precise corner point and mark each of the spots with a stake. Then stretch a line at the base of the stakes and use chalk or spray paint to mark the course of your wall.

Excavate for footings and for retaining walls, and include the drainage area (*review "Water Disposal," page 43*).

FOUNDATION

As you move your materials, you'll see why building mortared stone walls is heavy work. You'll also get an idea of why the foundation has to be strong.

FOOTINGS should be as thick as the wall, twice as wide, and deep as local codes specify. Lay in a 4-inch gravel base; level and tamp it.

REINFORCEMENT: In areas subject to frost heave, strong winds, or earthquakes, use rebar to strengthen any wall more than 3 feet high. Lay rebar along its length on each side and drive vertical lengths into the ground, leaving at least 2 feet exposed.

Pour the concrete and allow it to cure for a week. While it cures, you can prepare the rest of your materials.

COST CONTROL

You can cut your costs by filling the core of the wall with less attractive stones than those used on the wall's face.

To avoid wasted mortar, adjust batch sizes to the amount you can use in two hours. When laying a stone wall, the consistency of the mortar must be thick enough to support the weight of the stones without displacing the mortar.

SORT THE STONE

While the footings cure, sort the stones by size and appearance.

■ The largest will form the first course; graduating to smaller stones as the wall rises.

■ The most attractive will be face stone, prominent on the wall's most visible surface.

■ Ugly stones have a place, but it's on the less visible side of the finished wall.

■ Long, flat pieces make bond stones, to be set perpendicular to the face of the wall. They tie it together, from front to back.

■ Rubble, piddling little rocks, will be filler.

CLEANER IS STRONGER: Now that everything is sorted, lay the first course next to the footing. Wash the stones with a pressure sprayer. They must be free of soil and clay or the mortar won't stick to them.

Keep the hose handy. You'll need it for mixing mortar and to wet the stone if you're laying sandstone or absorbent fieldstone. These stones absorb moisture rapidly and wetting them will keep your mortar from drying prematurely. Nonabsorbent fieldstone and river rock don't need wetting.

MORTAR

Mortar comes in premixed bags—or make your own from masonry cement, adding sand and water in quantities specified on the bag.

MIXING: For a job as big as a wall, rent a power mixer (or try to convince your kids this is an opportunity to spend some quality time together). Even with a mixer, you'll need one helper just to mix and move the mortar.

BEDTIME: Use a mason's trowel to spread a bed of mortar on the footing. The bed must be thick enough (at least an inch) to fill the cracks between stones in the first course. Start the ends of your first course with bond stones.

MOVING UP: Once a course is laid, wait until the mortar sets slightly (to keep from dislodging it), then lay mortar and stone for the next course. Fit stones as snugly as possible. Fill gaps with small stones and lay a bond stone every 6 to 10 square feet.

STRIKING: Use a ½-inch dowel to smooth the joints between the stones. Then remove any residual mortar with a stiff brush. To avoid mortar stains on the stones, do not wash the wall until the mortar is completely set.

CURING: It takes between 3 to 7 days for a mortared wall to cure.

STRIKING AND FINISHING MORTAR

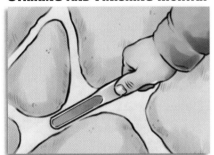

Cut off a broom handle or use a ½-inch dowel to smooth the setting mortar and to remove excess.

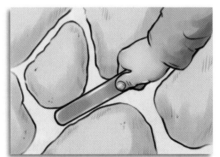

A metal jointing tool compresses the mortar tightly against the stones to make mortar/stone joints watertight.

After the joints are struck, use a stiff brush to clear away remaining mortar.

DRY IDEA: STACKING STONES WITHOUT MORTAR

If you're building a free-standing wall, dry-stacked stone is a useful option. The stones are held together by gravity and by friction, so their surfaces must bear snugly upon each other. Choose stones that fit together as tightly as possible.

To prevent the face stone from falling outward, both faces of a dry-laid stone wall should slant inward. To make a slope gauge, nail 1×4s together as shown, with the guide board slanted inward at a 15-degree angle.

Note that the stones are selected so that the inside edges slope downward toward the center of the wall. This transfers the weight of the stone to the center rather than to the faces of the wall which makes the wall more stable.

Set aside the longest stones for use as bond stones that will lock the stones together. (See page 50 for more information.)

CONCRETE BLOCK WALLS

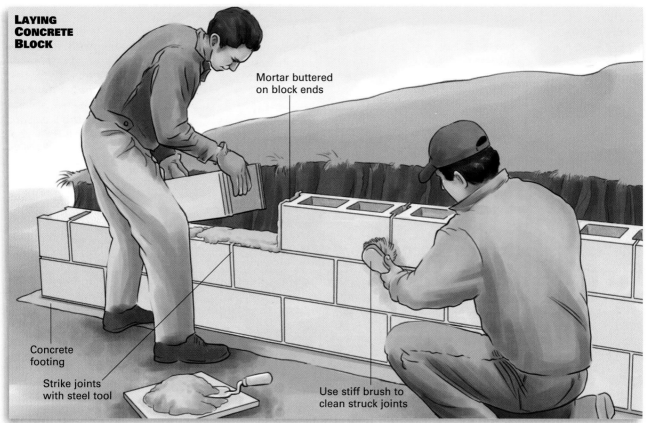

LAYING CONCRETE BLOCK

Mortar buttered on block ends

Concrete footing

Strike joints with steel tool

Use stiff brush to clean struck joints

Lay out the concrete blocks so the joints are staggered, as shown. For greater strength on high walls, use reinforcing wire in mortar between joints and fill the blocks with mortar.

Concrete block is inexpensive, durable, and relatively easy to install. And you can build in stages, working as your time permits. If you can't bring yourself to love the appearance of block, you can mask the wall with stucco or brick—or just use it in unobtrusive settings.

FOOTINGS FIRST

Lay out and excavate for footings as described on page 43. Use batter boards and mason's lines, squaring the corners as described. Footing standards are the same as for other walls—twice the width of the wall and deeper than the frost line (at least as deep as the wall's width).

REINFORCEMENT: Set rebar perpendicular to the footings to reinforce the wall against lateral or side pressure. About 8 inches from the bottom ends, bend the rebars to form a 90-degree angle and set the bent ends into the wet concrete. Place the rebar on 32-inch centers so they will extend up through the cores of the blocks.

ON THE LEVEL

Retaining walls must be level and plumb. Lay a uniform mortar bed so all joints will be ⅜-inch wide. Test each block for level and plumb. As needed, tap the blocks with the trowel handle to level the blocks.

To avoid injury while the footings are curing, tie red flags to the rebar tops.

BLOCK LAYOUT

Let the footings cure for at least three days, then lay out your first course without mortar. String the blocks along the footings, leaving ⅜-inch gaps (the width of the mortar joints). Limit the amount of cutting by using only full or half-blocks.

CUTTING BLOCKS: Mark a line on both faces of the block. Strike a mason's chisel lightly alone the line, working around both sides until the block splits.

MORTARING

A simple mortar formula for laying blocks is one part masonry cement and 2½ parts mason's sand, plus enough water to make a workable consistency. Test the mortar with a mason's trowel: Scoop up some mortar, shake off the excess, then turn the trowel over. If the mortar is right, it will stick to the trowel.

Using a mason's trowel, spread a full bed of mortar on the footings, about 1-inch thick and completely covering the course. Push the end blocks down until there is about ⅜ inch of mortar between the footing and the blocks. After setting the end blocks, fasten a mason's cord to align the intermediate blocks. Use a carpenter's level to make sure each block is level and plumb.

When you have completed the first course of blocks, lay reinforcing wire in the mortar to strengthen the joints.

Start succeeding courses at the corners so you have something to tie the mason's line onto. Constantly check for level and plumb as you proceed up the wall.

STRIKING: Press your thumb against the mortar joints; when the mortar is firm, use a jointing tool to strike the joints.

FILLING: After the blocks are laid, fill the cores that enclose the rebars with a high-slump (pourable) concrete mix (*see below*).

CAPPING

Cap the top of the wall to prevent water from entering the hollow blocks. The cap can be concrete or brick. If you want a concrete cap, stuff fiberglass insulation into the cores of the top blocks to keep the concrete from falling into the cores. Then trowel the concrete cap onto the top of the wall. Let the mortar cure for at least three days.

FILLING BLOCKS WITH CONCRETE

Filling block with concrete reinforces the wall. For commercial projects, special pilaster blocks are installed at intervals along the wall and filled with concrete. For most low walls, vertical steel rebar set in the concrete footings provide sufficient strength. The rebar is spaced 32 inches on center and run upwards through the hollow cores. When the wall is laid, mix concrete to a pourable consistency and fill the cores from the footings to the top.

As you lay up the block, use the edge of a mason's trowel to clean away excess mortar from the joints and scrape mortar splatters from the face of the blocks. If the wall will be left as is, this step should be carefully done; if the wall will be finished with stucco, you don't need to be as careful.

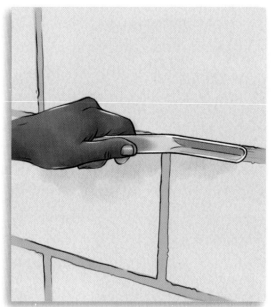

Now use a special steel jointing tool to strike or compress the mortar. Start with the horizontal joints. Forcing the mortar tight against the blocks forms a watertight seal.

Finish with the vertical joints. Jointing tools can remove small mortar lodges or particles that can trap and hold water. The jointing tools may have a tip that leaves either a concave or V-shaped joint that will shed water better than striking alone.

BRICK WALLS

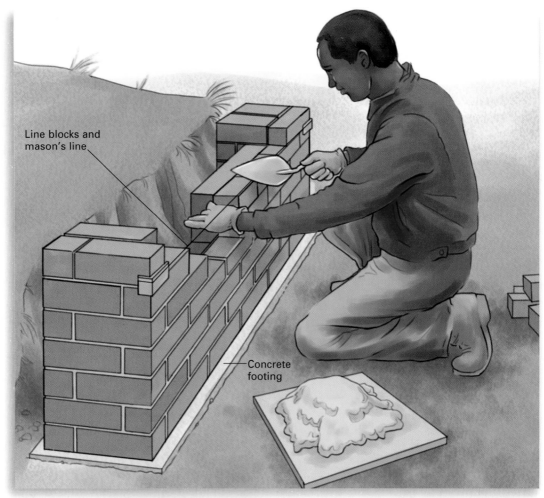

Lay a brick wall on a concrete footing. Note the line stretched between wood corner blocks as a guide to keep the courses straight. Walls more than a foot high require a double thickness of bricks.

Line blocks and mason's line

Concrete footing

The staggered pattern known as running bond is the most popular method of laying courses of brick. Use a carpenter's level or other straight edge to check brick alignment.

Check brick alignment with level

B rick can be laid in a wide variety of patterns: from flowing lines that fit informal landscapes to rectangular forms that accent formal styles.

FOOTINGS

If your wall is going to be no more than a foot high, such as a flower-bed border, you can lay it in a single row (one brick wide). Any wall higher than a foot should be laid in two rows (called wythes) with ⅜-inch spacing (the thickness of a mortar joint) between. Laid with these dimensions, a wall can be spanned with a one-brick header.

Set the wall on concrete footings that are twice as wide as the wall and at least as deep as the wall's width (always deeper than the local frost line). Because soil varies, check with your local building department to be sure your footing construction conforms to local requirements.

Lay out, excavate, and pour footings as described on page 42. Include the drainage area for retaining walls (*see "Water Disposal," also on page 43*). Drive batter boards and square the corners with mason's lines. Excavate the soil to the depth of the footing plus a 4-inch gravel base. Make forms if necessary and install rebar along the length on both sides and vertically at 2-foot intervals if your wall will be more than 3 feet high. Pour the footings and let them cure three to seven days.

MORTAR

Mix mortar for brickwork with one part portland cement, ¼ part hydrated lime, and 3 parts sand (or 1 part portland cement, 1 part masonry cement and 6 parts sand). Add water gradually as you mix. It should be plastic, but not runny.

TEST MIX: Load up a mason's trowel; shake off the excess, then turn the trowel over. The mortar should cling to the trowel.

FIRST COURSE: When the footings are cured, chalk a line for the front edge of the first course. String the first course along the center of the footings so only full or half-bricks are used, to eliminate unnecessary cutting. Leave a ⅜-inch gap between bricks for the mortar joint. Mark the footings at the end of each brick to serve as a guide.

Trowel mortar on the footings about ¾-inch deep and make a furrow down the center of the bed to spread it. Lay the first course in parallel bricks, starting with the corners and working to the center.

SUCCEEDING COURSES: The arrangement of succeeding courses will depend on your choice of pattern (or bond). For a running bond, start the second and alternate courses with a half-brick. Lay the corners five courses high so you have something to hold the line that will help you keep the courses straight.

Continue laying the bricks from both ends toward the middle, buttering the end of each brick before putting it in place. Then set the brick in the mortar and press it in position.

Be careful to maintain both the vertical and horizontal mortar joints at a ⅜-inch thickness. Use a level to check the bricks for level and plumb, and remove excess mortar with the edge of the trowel.

CLOSURE: Install the closure or last brick in the course at the middle of the wall. Butter both ends of the closure brick with mortar and set it straight down in the gap. When you finish the wall, cap it with a course of bricks laid on edge so no holes are showing.

If the brick wall is a retaining wall, install the drainage features discussed on page 43.

BRICKLAYING TECHNIQUE

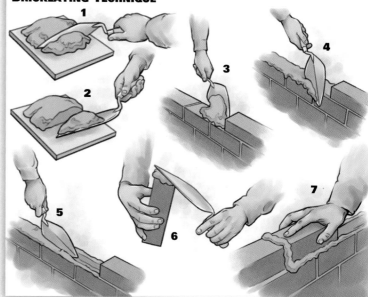

Follow these steps when laying brick: 1) Cut mortar from mortarboard. 2) Pick up mortar with a snapping motion. 3) Throw mortar with a sweeping motion and spread it evenly. 4) Cut off excess. 5) Lightly furrow the center of the bed. 6) Butter the ends of the brick with mortar using a sharp downward motion. 7) Shove the brick in place to force the mortar out of the joint.

GREAT WALL OPTIONS

The appearance of any wall can be enhanced by special features. For example, a brick or stone wall can incorporate a flower bed or planter, or can enclose a waterfall that spills into a pool below.

To build a fountain or waterfall, buy a low-voltage electric pump at your home or garden center. For planting flowers or ground cover plants such as ivy, interrupt dry stone or timber at random points with exposed soil.

Brick can be laid in many patterns—standard running bond, common bond, or English bond, or regular patterns can be altered to produce striking effects. At left, protruding headers and pop-out stretchers add pattern, texture, and shadow to the wall.

A variety of unique and attractive brick patterns can be achieved with careful planning and layout. Test your pattern by dry-laying the bricks first, and be sure any divisions are multiples of the brick width and/or length.

OTHER STONE WALLS

A dry-stacked stone wall is held upright by careful placement of the stones, with the effect of gravity. Note the slope on the face of the wall: The wall stones lean against the gravel and soil behind them. Note the perforated drainpipe below and behind the wall, and the gravel fill that must be added as the wall rises.

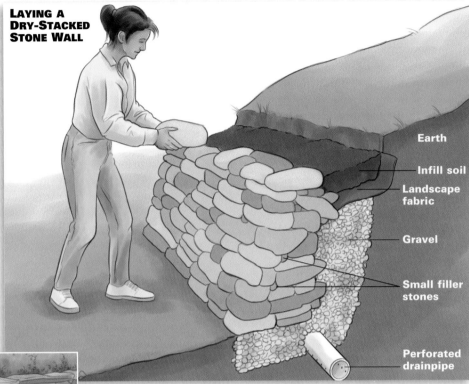

LAYING A DRY-STACKED STONE WALL

Earth

Infill soil

Landscape fabric

Gravel

Small filler stones

Perforated drainpipe

Build a concrete wall (see page 46) and use mortar, thin flagstone, or slate as a veneer. Lay the stones on the ground to establish a pattern, then transfer them to the mortared wall.

A dry-stacked (or dry-laid) stone wall, also called a gravity wall, requires patience and care. Centuries-old walls in New England, long overgrown, stand in testimony to the skill of their builders.

Because the stones are laid without mortar, the wall can go up quickly. To ease the load, have a work crew on hand to help. Heavy boots and durable gloves are essential to avoid injury and its attendant colorful language.

LANDSCAPE FABRIC

Landscape fabric lets water pass through but blocks weeds or grass from growing. Use it to prevent vegetation growth through a retaining wall, under a deck, a dry-laid walk, or patio. Landscape fabric is an excellent weed barrier for foundation plantings or flower gardens. Remove any existing vegetation, lay down the fabric, then cut holes where you will plant flowers. To conceal the fabric, cover it with bark or decorative stone.

SHOPPING FOR STONE

Take the measurements of your wall to your garden center or outdoor landscaping specialist. The dealer can help estimate the amount of stone you will need. When you shop for stone, remember that round boulders are the most difficult to lay because they do not align well to the course below. Flat stones are much easier to stack and fit.

NO FOOTING REQUIRED

A dry-laid stone wall does not require footings. It will not crack from frost heave because it moves and settles with—not against—the frost, making it a good choice for cold climates. However, it does require drainage. Dig a trench at least 1 foot deep— check with your building department for soil conditions and excavation requirements in your area—and pour and tamp a 6-inch gravel or crushed-stone base.

If you're building a retaining wall, you will also have to cut into the slope—either straight or at the same angle as the finished face will be (*see "Angling the Face," opposite*).

Lay out the footing excavation with batter boards and mason's line, squaring the corners by measuring off a 3-4-5 triangle (*see "Laying out a Wall," page 42*).

Excavate the footing trench to the depth required by local codes and lay the gravel bed. Level the bed and tamp it firmly.

PREPARATION

After you have dug and laid the bed with gravel, sort the stones by size and shape. Use a wheelbarrow to move the sorted piles along the length of the wall. You will use the largest stones for the bottom courses and smaller stones for filler.

As you're sorting, set aside the longest stones for bonding (they will tie the wall together perpendicularly) and make a pile of the broadest ones for cap stones.

ANGLING THE FACE

Because only gravity and friction hold the stones in place, the face of a free-standing wall must be sloped (or battered) to carry the weight. Each succeeding course must be set back about 2 inches for every vertical foot. The face of each course must slant toward the center (or the slope on a retaining wall).

SLOPE GAUGE: Use 1×4 lumber to build a slope gauge *(right)* to check the wall as you lay the stones. Set the angle, then nail a brace between the boards to hold them in place. See page 43 for another type of simple slope gauge.

Slope gauge

MAKING THE WALL

Start with bonding stones at the ends of the wall, then fill in toward the center, keeping the front edges of the stones at a slight slant toward the center. Use the slope gauge you've built—it will help you keep the angle consistent. Select stones that fit together as tightly as possible. Because it's gravity and friction that hold the wall together, each stone should have maximum contact and surface bearing on the one below. Use small stones to fill any gaps and to stabilize the large stones. Lay another bonding stone perpendicular to the face of the wall at least every 6 to 10 square feet. Bonding stones lock the wall together front to back.

RETAINING WALLS

If you're building a retaining wall, you can excavate the side of the slope to the desired angle. Also, excavate the drainage trench for gravel and perforated drainpipe *(see illustration on the opposite page)*.

After you lay the first course of stone, put landscape fabric behind it and fill the space between the wall and the slope with gravel. If the fabric is as long as the height of the wall, you can pull it up with each succeeding course, backfilling with gravel as you go. Landscape fabric will keep grass and weeds from growing between the stones, and it will let water drain out and keep the soil from washing through it.

TOOL LIST

Tools needed for wall construction include a trenching and a square-end shovel, a garden rake, a level, mason's line, a wheelbarrow, a brickset or mason's chisel for cutting stone, a mason's hammer, and a trowel to work the mortar. A garden tiller is useful for digging trenches. Use the tiller to loosen the soil, then remove the soil with a shovel.

ESTIMATING MORTAR MATERIALS

Dealers can help you estimate your needs if you provide measurements and material preferences. They can also calculate the amount and cost of cement, mortar, and landscape fabric.

■ **AREA:** You can get a rough idea of some materials yourself, using a tape measure and pencil. Concrete block, brick, and landscape timbers have uniform dimensions, so it's simple to estimate how much of these materials you'll need. Here's how: Multiply the length and height of your wall to get its area in square feet. Then divide that total area by the dimensions of one piece of

the material—one block, for instance—for a rough estimate of the number of pieces in the face of the wall. Remember to double that number if your wall is thicker than a single block or brick.

■ **WEIGHT:** Estimating stone is more difficult. Round stone is sold by weight: Eighty 25-pound stones make a ton. Your dealer can estimate the amount needed from the dimensions of your project.

These materials are too heavy to haul in a pickup. Have them delivered. Stone and brick are shipped on pallets and lifted with a hydraulic arm.

PRECAST BLOCK WALLS

Precast concrete planters are available in earth tones. They can retain the earth hill behind and be filled with soil and foliage to decorate the hillside.

Precast block expands the capabilities of landscape designers and puts wall-building within the reach of the homeowner. Attractive and effective, they're especially useful as retaining walls.

BEAUTY AND BRAWN

If the convenience of plain concrete block doesn't offset its utilitarian appearance, precast block offers a genuinely attractive alternative. Decorative block has the color, texture, and shape to simulate natural stone. Some are cast in shapes that add expression to the face of the wall.

One type of precast block has alignment holes positioned to take the guesswork out of assembly. Others have interlocking lips that align the blocks and secure them in place.

EASY ASSEMBLY

No footings are required for precast block installation. Simply dig a trench and pour, level, and tamp a 4- to 6-inch gravel bed. To assemble, stack the blocks in tiers, interlocking their joints—or drive rebar through the alignment holes into the soil at the base of the wall. Some models require fiberglass pins to lock the stones together.

GREEN WALLS

Blocks cast in the shape of oversized flower pots can be used to construct planted or "green" walls. Simply remove soil to position and level the blocks and fill the planting area with the soil. Stairstep your design up the slope face and plant flowers or ground cover.

Most blocks are manufactured for local consumption because of the shipping weight of these products. Look under "Concrete Products" in the yellow pages of your phone book to find a manufacturer in your area.

PRECAST WALL PLANTERS

4" perforated drainpipe

Interlocking blocks

Gravel for drainage

CANTILEVERED WALLS

The cantilevered or poured-concrete retaining wall requires forming and placing a large amount of concrete, so consider hiring a contractor to build it.

The process involves inserting rebar horizontally in the concrete footing. It will help support the heavy wall. Other rebars are bent at a 90-degree angle and wired in place before the footing is poured. Then the vertical rebar are wired to horizontal rebar every 12 inches from the footing to the top of the wall. Forms are assembled at the front and back sides of the wall, and concrete is poured into the forms. When the concrete wall has cured, the forms are removed and gravel is filled into the space between the wall and the earth slope. A perforated drainpipe laid near the footing provides drainage behind the wall. The top foot of the wall is backfilled with soil.

Note that the footing is stabilized by earth fill on the front face and by the weight of gravel and earth on the back side of the wall.

If the wall is more than 3 feet high, the concrete forms need to be set so the base of the wall is thicker than the top and the face of the wall slants back toward the sloped soil.

TIMBER WALLS

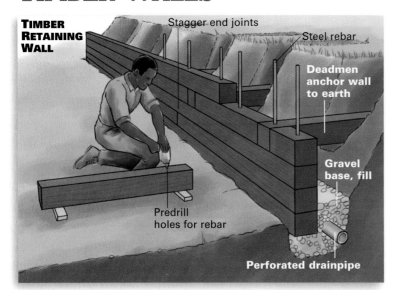

TIMBER RETAINING WALL

Stagger end joints

Steel rebar

Deadmen anchor wall to earth

Gravel base, fill

Predrill holes for rebar

Perforated drainpipe

The first course of timbers is installed below grade. Use a chain saw to cut timbers as needed. The timbers rest upon a level bed of gravel. Position a perforated drain pipe at footing level, sloped ⅛ inch per foot toward a storm drain or dry well (a hole filled with crushed rock). Lay landscape fabric over the drainpipe to prevent silt from plugging the drain holes. When the deadmen (see below) are in place, fill the area behind the timber wall with gravel.

Timber retaining walls, once built of railroad ties, now are most often made with commercial landscape timbers, treated to resist moisture and insects.

ASSEMBLY

No footings are needed. Dig a trench about a foot deep and shovel in 6 inches of gravel for drainage. Wet, tamp, and level the gravel before laying the first course of timbers.

■ Drill ½-inch holes down through the base timbers and drive 18-inch rebar into the soil. Be sure the timbers are level along their length and across their width.

■ Position the second course of timbers so its front edge is ½ inch behind the front face of the first course. Stagger the joints.

■ Drill 1-inch weep holes every 2 feet in the second course—or leave slight gaps at each joint—to provide drainage through the wall.

■ Drill ¼-inch holes at each end and at 2-foot intervals along the length of the timbers. Drive 10-inch barn spikes into the holes.

■ Continue laying up courses, each set back ½ inch from the one below it. Check often to be sure timbers are plumb and level.

For stability, cut 4-foot timbers as deadmen (timbers set into the slope perpendicular to the wall). Dig trenches in the soil behind the wall and install the deadmen (*above and right*). Install deadmen at 4-foot intervals, at depths of 6 to 12 inches below the grade.

SAFETY PRECAUTIONS: Wear heavy boots, leather-faced gloves, and protective eye glasses. Use a sharp chain saw to cut timbers and a 2-pound sledge or mash hammer to drive the spikes that hold timbers together.

DEADMEN (OVERHEAD VIEW)

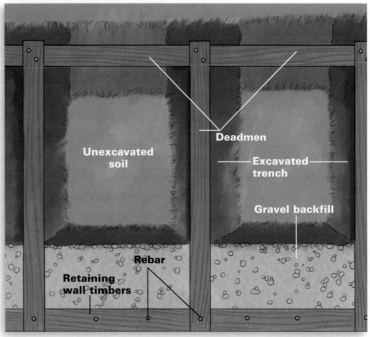

Deadmen

Unexcavated soil

Excavated trench

Gravel backfill

Rebar

Retaining wall timbers

MAINTAINING TIMBERS

Termites and carpenter ants will consume a lightly-treated timber wall. Buy .40-grade treated timbers for protection against them. Check the wall periodically for signs of insect infestation and use an aerosol insecticide to keep insects away. When the wall darkens with mildew and dirt, use a deck cleaner to clean it. Once a year, use a sprayer to apply a clear wood sealer to exposed wood.

Put deadmen— timbers set perpendicular to, and ends flush with the wall face—every 4 feet, at depths one or two timbers (6 to 12 inches) below grade or below the top of the wall. Deadmen anchor the top of the wall, to resist pressure from water or frost heave.

PATHS, WALKS, & DRIVEWAYS

Well-planned walks and driveways help unify the other elements of your landscape. They link the structures, separate the lawn and garden areas, and guide you from one place to another.

The materials you use and the way you shape their design contribute to the type of welcome your visitors sense. That first impression—curb appeal, as the real estate agents say—can significantly affect your home's value as well as its appearance.

When choosing materials for your walks, paths, and driveway, consider first the visual impact. There is an obvious difference between the functionality of concrete and the warmth of wood chips, and between the rustic look of cobblestone and the formality of pavers. As you'll see in this chapter, each material also requires a different level of maintenance and each has limits to its practicality. Balance the effect you want with your budget and the long-term upkeep the material will require.

Can you do it yourself? For most projects, the answer is yes. Brick and stone walks laid with mortar or set in sand are within the practical reach of most homeowners. Concrete or asphalt drives are better left to contractors.

The pathway color blends with the walls of the house to produce a monochromatic color scheme. Green foliage provides contrast.

Spread between curving, poured-concrete borders, the red rock walk adds color and texture that sets off the color of the house.

Sunlight streams through the openings in the rear wall to create an ever-changing pattern on the surface of this brick-faced porch.

This river-stone path borders a flower garden and provides access for tending the flowers or gathering a summer bouquet.

This large circular brick drive can hold many parked cars when the owners are entertaining. The circular pattern permits drivers to head onto the street safely rather than backing into traffic. The edged island is showcased by the drive to provide visual relief from the brick-paved expanse.

PATHS & WALKWAYS

A modest investment in paths and walkways can lead to a stunning improvement in your yard's appeal. Stone- or brick-in-mortar walks are certainly more expensive than poured concrete—but often not prohibitively so. If you amortize the cost over 10 or 20 years, you get a more accurate perspective of the cost of quality design. A high initial cost may pay off in the long run.

SAVING MONEY

Low-cost natural, durable, and attractive materials—pea rock, gravel, wood rounds, and stepping stones—can produce a walkway that is every bit as appealing as more expensive alternatives.

Build an inexpensive path of concrete stepping stones with an aggregate finish. Pour them yourself in homemade wooden forms (*see "Making Stepping Stones," page 62*). A pathway of wood chips or bark, winding through a flower garden, produces a harmonious effect at low cost. Depending on where you live and the availability of wood products, a short pathway of this type could be made in a single day for less than $200. (*For more information on making soft paths, see "Natural, Soft Paths," page 62.*)

EXCAVATING FOOTINGS

Use mason's line and stakes to establish the perimeter of the excavation. Dig footings and remove excess soil.

CUTTING STONE

First, mark the stone to be cut. Use an adjoining stone as a pattern, tracing the outline in pencil.

Next, position a mason's chisel on the cut line and strike the chisel with repeated blows along the line.

Finally, lay the stone over a pipe and strike the etched cut line to break away the waste.

MAKING YOUR BED

Whatever material you've chosen, the steps to prepare the bed will be similar.

HOW WIDE? A comfortable backyard path should be at least 3 feet wide. Walks leading to the front door should be wider to allow two people to walk side by side.

If you're planning to lay brick or other modular material, make the width an even multiple of its dimensions so you won't have to cut odd-size pieces.

Add ⅛ to ½ inch per course to your planned width to allow for sand or mortar joints—and add the width of your forms.

LAYOUT: First, lay out the rough edge of the walk with a garden hose. If your design is free form, mark one edge with chalk or spray paint. Use dowels cut to the width of your walk to trace the shape from your chalk line to the opposite side of the path.

For a straight walk, use batter boards to make the edge precise (*see "Laying out a Wall," page 42*).

EXCAVATE: Before you dig, decide how deep the bed will be. Use this guide to excavate for various materials:

■ **Mulch or gravel:** 6 inches (1 to 2 inches of sand and 4 inches of mulch or gravel).

■ **Brick or stone in sand:** 8 to 9 inches

(4 inches of gravel base, 2 inches of sand, and 2 to 3 inches of brick or stone).

■ **Poured concrete:** 8 inches (4 inches of gravel base and 4 inches of concrete).

■ **Mortared brick or stone:** 10½ to 12 inches (8 inches of gravel and concrete base, ½ to 1 inch mortar bed, and 2 to 3 inches of brick or stone).

If you want the finished grade of the walk to be above the level of the soil, subtract an

TWO WAYS TO SET STONE

Stone walks can be set dry or in mortar.

To dry-set stone, measure and mark out the perimeter of the walk and use a flat shovel to remove the sod from the area. Cover the area with landscape fabric to prevent vegetation growth between the cracks. Spread sand or gravel to a depth of 3 or more inches to level the area. Lay the stones either to serve as stepping stones with spaces between, or fit the stones together as closely as possible if that is the desired effect. Spread sand in the joints between the stones. Concrete pavers, shown here, can also be dry set in the same fashion. Tap the pavers in place with a rubber mallet.

To build a mortared stone walk, you must excavate the area and build wooden forms along the perimeter. Excavate the area deep enough to include a 4-inch layer of gravel for drainage, a 4-inch concrete pad, plus the thickness of the mortar and stone. When the concrete has cured for three days, apply a 1-inch mortar coat on the concrete base. Level the stones in the mortar and let cure for at least one day. Then use a mason's trowel or mortar bag to fill the joints with mortar.

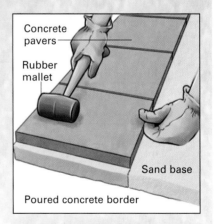

Concrete pavers

Rubber mallet

Sand base

Poured concrete border

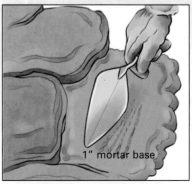

1" mortar base

PATHS & WALKWAYS
continued

The steps for laying a dry-brick path include excavation, installing permanent edging, placing the sand base, laying the brick, and sweeping sand into the joints. The permanent edging can be redwood, cedar, or mortared brick or stone. Drive the edging stakes below the surface of the turf and cover them with soil. Edging holds the bricks in place; sand in the joints stabilizes them.

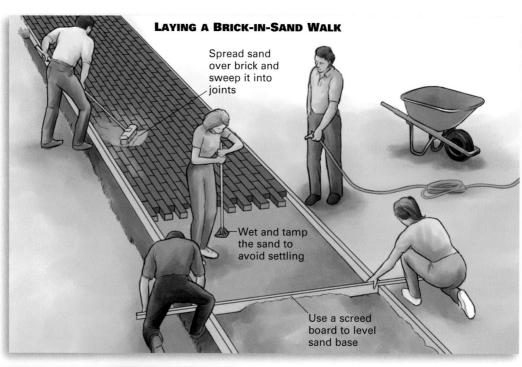

LAYING A BRICK-IN-SAND WALK

Spread sand over brick and sweep it into joints

Wet and tamp the sand to avoid settling

Use a screed board to level sand base

Use a home-made screed to level the sand base for a dry-set walk. Notch a 2x4 as shown so its bottom edge is as deep as the thickness of your brick, and pull it across your forms.

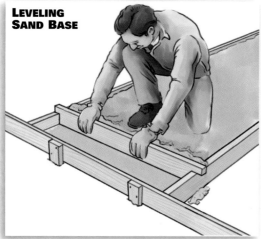

LEVELING SAND BASE

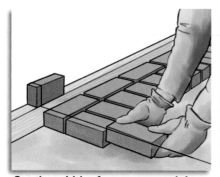

Set the width of permanent edging to avoid cutting brick. Wet and tamp the sand base to pack it tight. Use a mason's line as a guide to level the brick as you set them.

Set and level the brick with a rubber mallet. Fill joints with sand to stabilize the brick. Then wet and tamp the surface.

inch from the depths above. That will set your walk slightly above soil level, which will let water run off and allow you to mow the edges without having to trim them separately.

Dig out the turf with a square shovel. Loosen the soil with a rototiller and excavate to the proper depth. Use the sod to patch other areas and use the soil to level low spots.

SET FORMS OR EDGING: Once the digging is done, build forms for any project that requires concrete, or install any edging you plan to use. Drop the mason's line to the final grade of the walk and lay in pavers, timbers, or forms that will hold the concrete.

FINISH THE BED: Pour, tamp, and level your bedding material—dampened sand or gravel and sand, depending on the installation. The bed provides support, drainage, and protection from frost heave for concrete or mortared projects. For all walks except poured concrete ones, cover the first layer of the bedding materials with landscape fabric to discourage vegetation growth.

LAYING BRICK AND STONE

If you're using wood chips, bark, mulch, or crushed stone, all you have to do is pour, tamp, and level. Brick or stone set in sand require a few more steps, as do concrete and mortared surfaces.

DRY-SET: For a stone walk set in sand, lay all the stone in place. For brick or concrete pavers, start at the corners and lay the edging

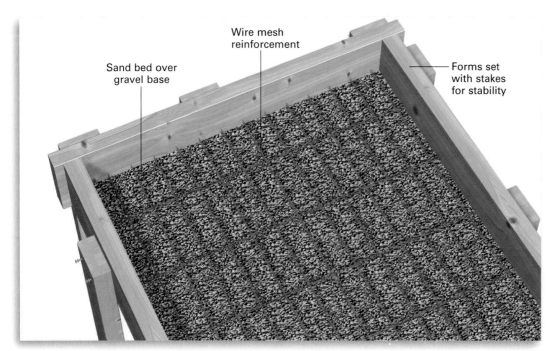

Sand bed over gravel base

Wire mesh reinforcement

Forms set with stakes for stability

When setting forms for a concrete slab, coat the inside faces with wood sealer to prevent the concrete from sticking. Use duplex (double-head) nails or exterior screws to temporarily secure the stakes and forms in place. With the gravel base poured and covered by the wire reinforcing mesh, you're ready to pour.

first, spacing the bricks about ⅛-inch apart (many pavers come with tabs that keep the proper spacing). Use a rubber mallet to tap the material in place, and check for level with a 2×4 as you go. Tap down high spots and fill in low ones. When the surface is laid, sweep mason's sand to fill the spaces, wet the surface slightly, and use a power tamper to force the sand into the cracks.

POURED OR MORTARED: You are pouring a sidewalk in each of these projects, but mortared surfaces are concealed by the top layer of stone, brick, or other paving material.

The concrete is poured over a gravel base, as described earlier. For strength, lay reinforcing wire in the excavation, supported on bricks every 4 square feet. Pour the concrete and level it with a span of 2×4. Finished surfaces will need to be smoothed with a float; the bed of a mortared surface is best left rough.

If you are laying brick or stone, let the concrete pad cure for at least three days. Then spread a mortar base (½ inch for brick, 1 inch for stone) and push the material into it. You can purchase plastic spacers designed to space the bricks evenly.

Wait 24 hours and use a mortar bag to grout the joints, being careful to keep it off the faces of the brick. When the mortar is firm, use a jointing tool to smooth the joints. After about three hours, use wet burlap to clean away excess mortar.

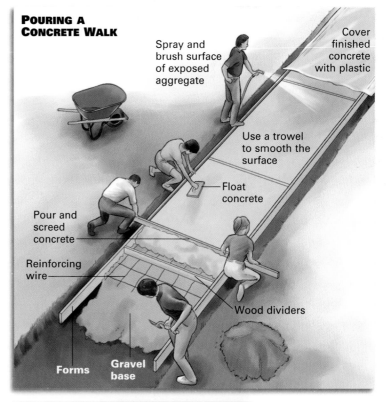

POURING A CONCRETE WALK

Spray and brush surface of exposed aggregate

Cover finished concrete with plastic

Use a trowel to smooth the surface

Float concrete

Pour and screed concrete

Reinforcing wire

Wood dividers

Forms

Gravel base

A brick drive adds a sense of luxury and permanence to your property. Consider hiring a masonry contractor when planning an extensive project like this.

STEPS

Steps can climb straight up a slope, curve around it, or zigzag—especially useful to break up a long or steep rise. Like the rest of your walkway, steps can be built of concrete, brick, timbers, flagstones—even loose material like gravel or wood chips.

RISE AND RUN

If you have a long flight of steps, do not try to build one straight flight. Check the lay of the land and lay out a natural path, following the land contour. Build the steps to zigzag up the hill, with landings where the steps change direction.

To lay out the steps, you must first determine the rise and the run of the span. On short runs, stand a 2×4 upright where you want the bottom step to start. Clamp another 2×4 to it horizontally, level with where the steps will peak. Now measure along the 2×4s from their intersection. The height is the rise; the distance across is the run.

On a longer series of steps, anchor a line at the top of the rise and use a line level to hold it level. Drop a plumb bob to the bottom of the run. With a helper, measure the height (the rise) and the span (the run).

RISERS AND TREADS

You need the rise and run measurements to calculate the height and depth of each step. Steps can be 4 to 8 inches high, but 5 to 7 inches is usually the most comfortable.

To calculate the number of steps, divide the total rise by the step height you want, rounding fractions up. For example, if the slope is 48 inches high and you want 7-inch risers (step heights), you will have seven of them.

Treads—the top surface of the steps—should be at least 11 inches deep for safety and comfort. For evenly spaced treads, divide the run by the number of risers you've calculated. For example, seven treads on an 84-inch run would each be 12 inches deep. Steps should be at least 2 feet wide (4 feet is average). Where you want to allow two people to walk comfortably side by side, give them enough shoulder room—build the steps 5 feet wide.

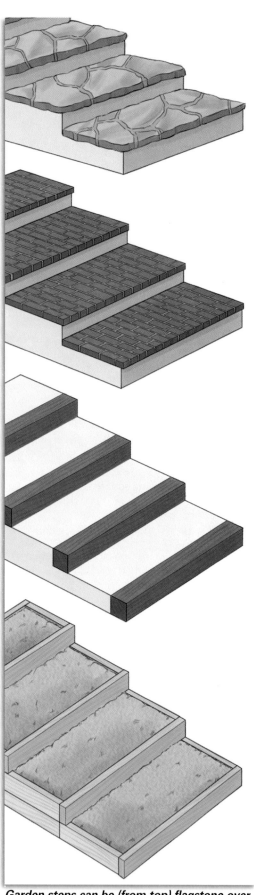

Garden steps can be (from top) flagstone over concrete, brick, concrete with timber edging, or timbers with gravel.

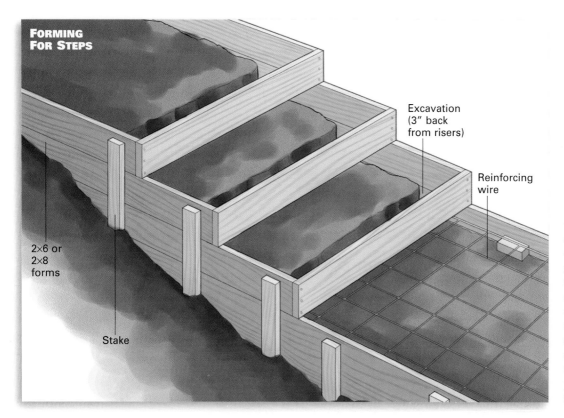

FORMING FOR STEPS

Excavation (3" back from risers)

Reinforcing wire

2×6 or 2×8 forms

Stake

Use 2×6 or 2×8 lumber to build step forms for pouring concrete. Before assembling the lumber, spray a clear wood sealer on the inside faces of the boards so you can remove the forms easily.

CONSTRUCTION

Drive stakes to mark the corners of your stairway. Use a framing square to test the corners, then mark the course of the stairs with chalk or paint.

Remove the sod and dig out the rough perimeter of your stairs. Excavation depths vary, depending on your construction materials (*see page 57*). Most steps need a level bed of 4 to 6 inches of gravel or sand for stability. For example, masonry steps need a 4-inch gravel base and 4 inches of concrete, poured into wooden forms (*above*).

FOR MORTARED STEPS, make sure the forms include the riser heights, the concrete base, the ½- to 1-inch mortar, and the thickness of the bricks or stone surfacing material you will lay.

IF YOU INSTALL TIMBER RISERS, set them in a 4-inch gravel base. Drill ½-inch-diameter holes down through the timbers, about 1 inch from each end. Then drive 24-inch rebars into the earth beneath.

You can build the treads two timbers deep, each anchored by rods, or excavate the area behind the timbers and fill it with gravel, bark, concrete, or brick laid in sand.

Install the tread material using the same techniques as for paths and walkways (*see pages 56–59*).

FIGURING RISE AND RUN

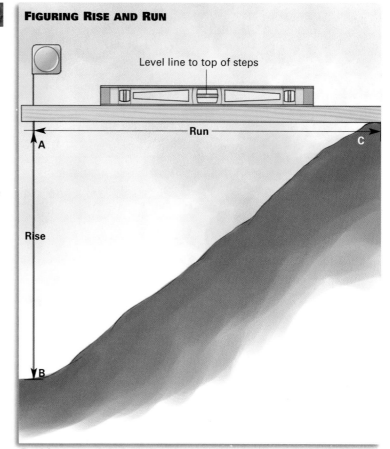

Level line to top of steps

Run

A

C

Rise

B

Position a straight board at the top of the slope and have an assistant hold it level. The distance between points A and B is the rise of your stairs. The distance between points A and C is called the run. Round both distances up to the nearest inch.

NATURAL, SOFT PATHS

Natural materials make attractive, low-cost pathways, and the variety of materials available may surprise you. Natural materials include redwood bark or wood chips of other species, crushed granite, redrock, or a rainbow of decorative stone.

PURCHASING MATERIALS

Redwood or cedar bark and chips are available in bags from your neighborhood home center. In many areas, you can also purchase pine needles in bulk. Local parks often recycle wood chips from the trees they remove. You can often have them for the hauling.

Decorative stone is also sold in bags. But if your path will require large quantities of stone, it will be cheaper to buy it in bulk. Depending on where you live, a nearby granite works or stone quarry may be able to offer you ton-lot prices.

MAKING STEPPING STONES

To make concrete stepping stones, first build forms of 2×4s. Build them in squares, to make things easy, or in other shapes if you feel creative. Hinge the corners and close one with a hook—the forms will come away easily once they're set. Seal the forms with clear sealer to help them "let go" of the cured concrete. Set the forms on plywood, pour the concrete, level it, and let it cure. Add a layer of crushed stone or pea gravel for texture.

MAKING THE PATH

To create a soft path, lay it out and excavate as described on pages 56 to 59. Excavate to a depth of 6 inches, and lay in timber forms or other edging. If the pathway borders a garden, you won't need permanent edging. But if it runs through a lawn, install brick or wooden edging to contain the gravel or chips.

Next, pour a 2-inch sand base, then level and tamp it. Put landscape fabric over the sand to prevent weed growth. Then spread and level the stones or wood chips.

ALTERNATIVES

Loose materials can be combined with stepping stones—either natural stones such as flagstones or concrete rounds. Concrete rounds come in many sizes and colors. You can even make your own (see "Making Stepping Stones," left). An aggregate stone surface will complement your path better than stones with smooth surfaces. Place the stones about 2 feet apart.

An alternative to stepping stones, wood rounds may be a weather-resistant species, such as redwood or cedar, or any durable wood species, such as oak. If you use wood rounds from your local lumber mill, apply three coats of clear wood sealer to all surfaces.

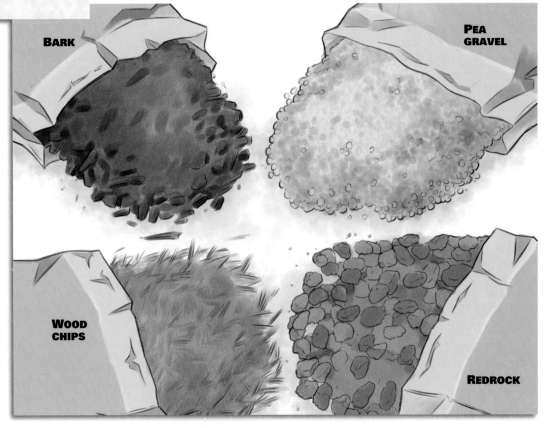

Loose materials for natural, soft paths come in bags or in bulk. You'll need plenty for your pathway: a layer at least 4 inches thick. Check with your local materials supplier or garden center for materials other than these that are native to your region.

BARK

PEA GRAVEL

WOOD CHIPS

REDROCK

DRIVEWAYS

This driveway combines an unusual variety of materials: The foreground is asphalt (blacktop) from the street to the property line, with brick paving beyond, all bordered by concrete edging.

Whether they're made of concrete or asphalt, driveways will likely be the most difficult job in your landscape. **LAYING ASPHALT** involves hot, hard work and heavy machinery—a job for a contractor. **BRICK OR INTERLOCKING PAVERS,** on the other hand, could be managed by a capable homeowner—but only with a large and experienced work crew. Like mortared pathways, pavers require a concrete base. **POURING CONCRETE** becomes much more difficult when the area reaches the scale of a driveway. But even if you hire crews to do the work, understanding the process will help you make better consumer decisions.

AMOUNTS

A single-car drive must be at least 10 feet—preferably 12 feet—wide so passengers can step from the car onto the slab. A double driveway should be 20 feet wide.

For car traffic, you'll need a concrete slab 4 inches thick. Got a truck? Bulk up that driveway; you'll need a 5- to 6-inch slab to support the extra weight.

Figure a cubic yard of concrete for every 81 square feet on a 4-inch slab. For a 5-inch slab, you'll need about 20 percent more; and for 6 inches, 50 percent more. The double drive shown (*right*) covers 700 square feet, not counting the turnaround wings, and requires nine cubic yards of concrete.

Concrete suppliers can prepare a mix blended for your specific use, with a slump (pourability) appropriate for the current weather conditions. They can even treat it (a process called "air entrainment") to resist cracking in cold weather.

EXCAVATION AND POURING

The site must be graded so the finished driveway slopes away from the garage or other adjacent buildings at a minimum rate of ¼-inch per running foot.

Concrete requires a gravel base equal to the slab thickness for drainage and support, so the excavation must be deep enough for the base and slab. If you decide to pour your own drive, tamp the base so it is well compacted. Lay 6×6-inch number-10 wire mesh over the gravel to strengthen the base. Support the mesh on bricks or blocks (called dobies) so it will stay centered in the poured slab.

Use a straight board that is longer than the width of the drive to level the concrete. Then smooth the slab with a bull float.

Let the concrete set until the surface sheen (bleed water) goes away. Kneel on 1×12s covered with scrap carpet while you trowel the slab. Then use an edging tool to round off—or relieve— the edges, then tool expansion grooves into the slab at 10-foot intervals. Cover the slab with sheet plastic to retard moisture loss during curing.

Build the drive wide enough so you can get out of your car without trampling the lawn. And consider a turnaround drive, which spares you from the perils of backing into traffic.

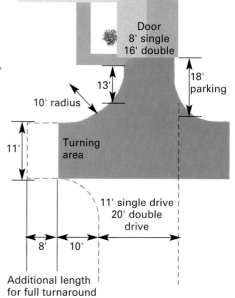

Door
8' single
16' double

13'

18' parking

10' radius

11'

Turning area

11' single drive
20' double drive

8'   10'

Additional length for full turnaround

DECKS, PATIOS, & SHADE STRUCTURES

For a minimum investment of time and money, outdoor structures such as decks, patios, and shady overheads can add value, comfort, and beauty to your landscape.

For example, a 12×12-foot ground-level deck of treated lumber can be built for less than $300, including fasteners and stain— and a simple overhead can cost even less.

Building structures involves some basic skills that are within the capabilities of even inexperienced homeowners. If you can follow simple plans, dig a hole, saw a board, and drive a nail, you can take on most of the projects described in this chapter.

Manufacturers of building materials have developed some innovative products to make building easier for the weekend do-it-yourselfer.

Screw-together step risers, for example, eliminate the carpenter's math that would otherwise be necessary to cut step stringers.

Pre-cut project packages provide all the materials for structures as elaborate as gazebos. Like giant hobby kits, they include every little fastener and full assembly instructions.

However, if you are planning a large or complicated project, such as a multi-level or second-story deck, think about hiring a pro to build it or to advise and assist you as you build.

Set just outside the kitchen door, this raised mini-platform deck provides an elevated view of the yard and adds an unusual architectural touch to the wider deck. The horseshoe-shape railing helps set off the deck even more dramatically. A clear sealer preserves the natural wood tone of the deck and railing.

A flagstone path leads to a rock waterfall and ground-level pool. Pool materials are available at garden centers. The park bench offers a sunny resting spot.

An overhead can provide full shade or partial sun, depending on the roof structure you select. Lattice, screening, or a fence can ensure privacy.

ANATOMY OF A DECK

The first step in building a deck is to familiarize yourself with the terms. So here's a quick deck-builder's dictionary:

BEAMS OR GIRDERS: Hefty framing members attached horizontally to the posts to support the deck structure.

DECKING BOARDS: Attached to the joists to form the floor of the deck.

JOISTS: Horizontal framing members that sit atop the beam or girder and support the decking boards. Joists can be either 16 or 24 inches *on center* (the distance between the centers of adjacent, parallel framing members in a series).

LATTICE: A grid-work of plastic or wood slats that conceals base framing and keeps out windblown debris while permitting free airflow for ventilation.

LEDGER: A horizontal support attached to the house to hold up one side of the deck.

PIERS: Masonry columns that support the posts and the structure above. They protect the posts from water and insect damage at ground level. On sites subject to frost heave, concrete is poured in a hole dug to frost depth. Consult your building department for frost depth in your area. Precast concrete piers may be set on shallower bases, or footings, where frost heave is not a factor.

POSTS: Timbers set on end (vertically) to support the structure above.

RISERS: Enclose the vertical spaces between stairway treads. As illustrated, risers are often omitted on deck and other exterior steps.

RAILS: Components that provide a safety barrier at the edges of the steps. Rails should be built so the handrail can be completely gripped by the person's hand, and should be securely attached so they are strong enough to support a falling person's weight.

RAILINGS: The horizontal timbers that extend from one deck post to another to form a safety barrier at the perimeter of the deck. The term is often used to refer to the entire rail structure, including posts, top rails, and balusters/spindles. The balusters, the smallest vertical components, are positioned to fill the space between the top and bottom rails and between rail posts. Minimum baluster spacing for child safety is four inches.

SKIRT BOARDS: Finished lumber that covers and finishes the exposed face of rough perimeter joists.

STRINGERS: The long wood components that support the weight of the step load and to which the treads are attached.

TREADS: The horizontal, stepping surfaces of a stairway.

Rafter

Beam

BASIC DECK CONSTRUCTION

Decking boards

Rim joist

Pier

Overhead
ledger

Deck ledger

Joist

Post

Top railing

Baluster

Rail

Tread

Post

Stringer

DESIGN AND PLANNING

When planning your deck, consider what size groups you will entertain, as well as ease of maintenance, accessibility, and whether the deck will be in the sun or shade when you use it most. Don't forget to provide electrical outlets for appliances.

EASE OF ACCESS

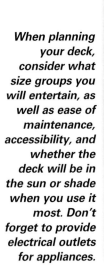

In the United States, one family in four has someone with a physical disability. Why not plan your deck so it can be enjoyed from the seat of a wheelchair? After all, that could very suddenly be the position of any one of us.

Instead of steps, a gentle ramp makes for easy walking or wheeling. The gentler the slope, the better—no more than one foot of rise for 12 feet of run. Build your ramp at least 42 inches wide—48 inches is better—to allow easy wheelchair passage. You'll also find it easier to move deck furniture and that jumbo barbeque grill you hope to add someday.

If the rise is high and you need a long run for a gentle slope, build a turn and platform every 12 feet. Use treated lumber and build sturdy side rails to prevent accidents.

Planning determines whether your deck project will be an orderly progression of stages or a chaotic series of crises. You can end up with a deck either way, but only by planning will you get the deck, the cost, and the experience you want.

The materials you choose, for instance, will determine how long your deck lasts and how much you'll spend for upkeep. Use pressure-treated lumber for the posts and joists—they are cheaper and have more strength than cedar or redwood.

Use the money saved for redwood or cedar deckboards, rails, and trim. Decking should be 2× or ⁵⁄₄ (which actually is 1 inch thick) lumber, no more than 6 inches wide. Wider stock is more likely to cup. Galvanized hardware and fasteners are a must. Though not required, metal hangers make stronger joints than toenailing.

INTEGRATE STYLES

Decks, like other outdoor structures, make an architectural statement, and your deck design will affect the overall impact of your home. **COMPLEMENT:** Integrate your deck design so that it complements the style of your home. For example, scallop the deck trim to match the gingerbread flavor of a Victorian-style home.

VIEWS: If your house overlooks a vista, take advantage of it with a second-story deck that recalls the walkways of large homes with an ocean view.

LINES: Enhance a modern- or ranch-style home with crisp straight lines, trimmed in stock dimension lumber.

SLOPES: Decks can solve problems with terrain. If your yard slopes steeply away at the back of the house, a deck creates a level outdoor entertainment area for less money and effort than excavating for a patio.

At some point, you may find yourself balancing deck design with your skills and budget. A simple square or rectangular deck, regardless of its size, is easiest for do-it-yourself construction. If you want a large deck that will wrap around two or more sides of the house, or if you plan a multi-level deck, your construction may require professional help.

HOW BIG?

The answer to the question about deck size lies in how you're going to use the space. If the deck will be just a family retreat, you can get by with modest dimensions—12×15 feet or so. If you frequently entertain groups, build it to accommodate the crowds. If you do both, be sure part of the deck space is isolated—under an overhead, behind a lattice screen, or on a different level. The total area will serve your parties and the isolated section will evoke an intimacy that your family will appreciate.

TRY IT OUT FOR SIZE: The scale of outdoor structures can fool you—what looks just right indoors will suddenly seem tiny outside. It's time to take a trial run to get the size that looks right in your landscape and also one that fits your entertaining needs.

Mark the proposed perimeter on the ground with a garden hose. Then move in the deck furniture, your barbecue grill, and any other items you expect to use. Consider the

scale of your project from different areas of your yard. Get the whole family together in the proposed area to see how spacious the deck will feel from the inside. Allow ample room so that people can move about freely within the area. If the space seems cramped, extend the lines until they're right for scale and comfort.

SPECIAL FEATURES

Most building codes require decks 30 or more inches above ground to have protective railing all around the perimeter. Be safe and smart by installing railings on any deck more than one step high.

SAFETY SECRET: The best solution may be safety disguised as seating: Built-in benches around the deck answer both needs without making anyone feel corralled by a nonstop railing.

Cantilevered seating extending from the edge of the deck gives guests a place to sit without taking up deck floor space. And perimeter seating costs only slightly more than railing.

HEALTHY OUTLETS: Don't forget electrical outlets and gas lines for comfort, cooking, and entertainment. You'll need wiring for lights and outlets for TVs, radios, electric cooking utensils, or any other equipment you intend to use on the deck. Installing them now won't cost as much as adding them later.

PLANS AND PERMITS

When you have decided on the design and size of your deck, draw up plans on graph paper (see "Dimensions and Details" page 18). Many building-supply centers can use a computer to draw the plans for you, complete with all details and a price list for materials. Use the plans to obtain a building permit from your building department, and keep a copy to guide you in building the deck.

MATERIALS MATTER

For any exterior structure, choose lumber that is resistant to decay and insect attack—naturally weather-resistant redwood, cedar, and cypress, or lumber that has been chemically treated (pressure-treated lumber) to resist decay. All fasteners must be aluminum or hot-dipped galvanized or double-galvanized steel. Fastener cost is a minor item in

your construction budget, so premium screws (with square heads and double-galvanized finishes) are best for exterior application. To avoid injury from popped deck board fasteners, blind-nail composite tongue-and-groove decking, or use metal deck connectors that secure the deck boards to the sides of the joists.

BUILDING A DECK

ATTACHING THE LEDGER

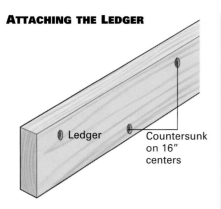

Ledger

Countersunk on 16" centers

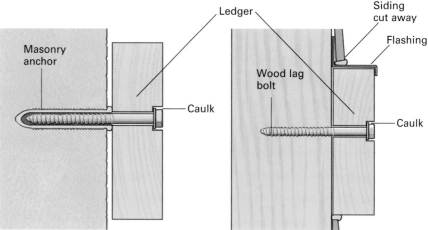

Masonry anchor

Caulk

Ledger

Siding cut away

Flashing

Wood lag bolt

Caulk

The ledger must be securely attached to the band joist (the rim of the house frame) to support the deck. Drive lag screws into the band joist to attach the ledger to wood walls. Use masonry anchors and lag bolts to attach the ledger to concrete or brick.

With plans and building permit in hand, it's time to go to work.

THE LEDGER BOARD

Mark the location of the ledger board on the side of the house, at least 2 inches below the access door. Be sure to allow for the thickness of the deck boards; they will rest on top of the ledger. Cut the ledger 3 inches shorter than the deck length to allow for framing members attached to its ends.

How you fasten the ledger depends on the surface of the house:

MASONRY: Using a hammer drill with self-threading masonry anchors, drill at each end of the ledger location and at 16-inch intervals along its length.

Drill recessed holes in the ledger at corresponding locations and secure it with ½-inch lag screws (5-inch length) and washers. Caulk the edges.

SIDING: Use your circular saw to cut away the siding where the ledger will go. The cut-out should be as long as the final length of the deck.

Drill holes with washer recesses in the ledger ends and at 16-inch intervals, staggering them to avoid splits along the grain. Prop the ledger against the wall and mark the holes by drilling lightly. Secure the ledger with ½×5-inch lag screws with washers. Caulk the joints to keep moisture out, and install flashing where the siding and the top of the ledger meet.

LAYOUT

Build batter boards from 2×4s and set them just outside the corners of the deck. Attach mason's lines at the center of post locations on the ledger and secure them to the batter boards, making sure the lines are level. Adjust the lines until the diagonal measurements are equal.

Confirm that corners are square with the "3-4-5" test: From a corner, mark one spot 3 feet out along the mason's line. On the ledger, mark a spot 4 feet from the corner. If the corner is square, the distance between your marks will be exactly 5 feet. Adjust your strings until it is.

SETTING DECK POSTS

To find the center of your post locations, drop a plumb bob at the intersection of your mason's lines.

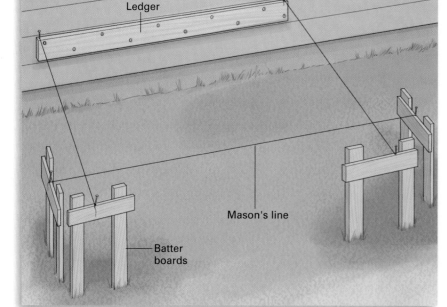

DECK LAYOUT

Ledger

Mason's line

Batter boards

DECK FRAMING

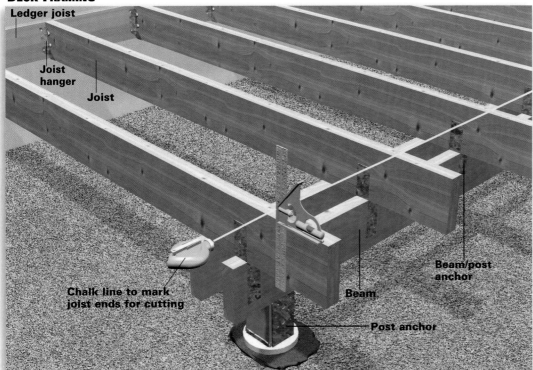

Ledger joist

Joist hanger

Joist

Chalk line to mark joist ends for cutting

Beam/post anchor

Beam

Post anchor

Attach the joists to the ledger with joist hangers, and beams to posts with beam/post hangers or seismic ties. After marking the joist ends, cut them and attach the header joist.

Dig holes (12 inches wide at the top and 18 inches at the bottom) 6 inches below the frost line for concrete piers. In poorly drained soil, dig an extra 4 inches for a gravel base.

Premixed concrete makes pier-pouring relatively easy and less time-consuming than mixing your own. Just add water gradually until the mix is pourable but not runny.

ABOVE-GRADE POSTS: You may either pour concrete to grade level and position a precast concrete pier on the wet concrete (3 inches above grade), or set form tubes. Hold the tubes in place with scrap wood so their tops are about 3 inches above grade. Surplus concrete at the bottom of the hole will make a footing. Center a J-bolt in the wet concrete (drop the plumb bob again to be exact) and level it. Let the concrete cure, backfill the holes, and attach post anchors.

POSTS BELOW GRADE: Setting posts below grade is easier with short posts—those that won't rise above deck level. After you've dug the post hole, tie your mason's lines 1¾ inches out from the original intersection. This will mark the outside edges of the post.

Put the post in the hole, plumb it with the intersecting lines, brace it, and pour the concrete. Check the post for plumb again, and slope the concrete so rainwater will run off. If your deck is low to the ground and will be screened with lattice, now's the time to remove the sod and lay landscape fabric to keep the vegetation in control.

BEAMS AND JOISTS

Using a water level, mark the posts at ledger height. For side-by-side beams, cut at the mark and use ½-inch lag screws and washers to attach the beams flush with the cut. For top-mounted beams, measure the beam width down and cut. Make top-mounted beams from doubled 2×10s with spacers of pressure-treated wood. On extended posts, attach the beams so the top is level with the bottom of the ledger. Install joists (crown up and on 16- or 24-inch centers) with joist hangers and hurricane ties, using angle brackets to attach the header to the front of the joists.

JOIST HANGERS

Because the ledger and deck joists are perpendicular, the only nailing technique for joining them is the toenailed joint. But toenailing produces a weak joint that may fail. To ensure maximum support, use metal joist hangers to join joists to ledgers or headers.

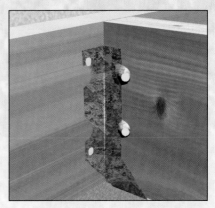

BUILDING A DECK
continued

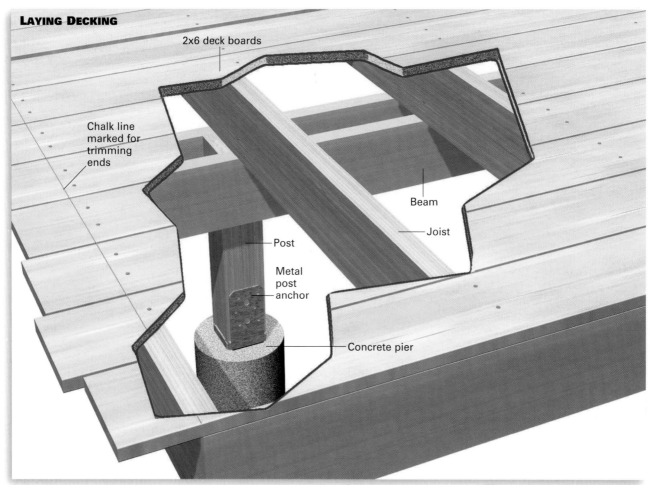

LAYING DECKING

2x6 deck boards

Chalk line
marked for
trimming
ends

Beam

Joist

Post

Metal
post
anchor

Concrete pier

FOUR DECKING PATTERNS

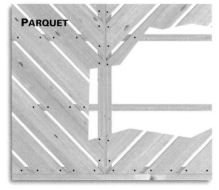

STANDARD

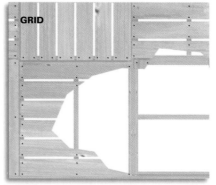

GRID

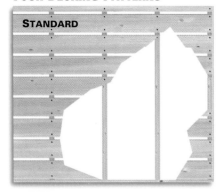

PARQUET

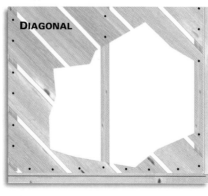

DIAGONAL

The superstructure or support framing of the deck includes the concrete post base, metal post connectors, 4×4 posts, beam, ledger joist (not shown), and deck joists. Because wider deck boards tend to cup and warp, use boards no more than 6 inches in width. Predrill nail holes to avoid splitting the deck boards. Use only two nails at joist locations, or conceal deck board fastening with metal connectors. Lay deck boards best side up.

Different decking patterns require different kinds of support. The more complicated they are, the more time and money they will require.

DECKING PATTERNS

You can install deck boards perpendicular to the joists, diagonally (such as at a 45-degree angle), or in a checkerboard pattern. Interesting patterns are unusual for two good reasons: difficulty and expense.

Diagonal and checkerboard installations require joists that are 12 inches on center, double joists, and extra braces. You'll also waste more decking lumber as you saw off odd ends.

Setting the decking at right angles to the joists is easier and more economical. But if you have the skills, patience, and budget to take on a more distinctive deck pattern, then your imagination is your only limit.

STARTING AND SPACING

Start with the board next to the house and attach it so it's parallel. Cut the first board to the proper length, but start—and finish—subsequent decking with an overhang.

Pressure-treated lumber will shrink in time, so butt its edges together. For other woods, space each row about ⅛-inch apart to allow for expansion and water drainage, using spacers or an 8d nail. Do a little math to see if a slightly thinner or wider space will keep the final board at a full width.

For years, professionals advised laying deck boards bark-side (outer growth rings) up, to reduce cupping and raised wood grain. Research has shown that although cupping and raised grain are reduced, boards placed bark-side up show greater checking and will warp anyway. Place the best-looking side up and protect it with water-repellent sealer.

END JOINTS

Use full-length boards where possible. If end joints are necessary, make sure they butt together over the center of the joists. You can increase their strength by first nailing 2×4 cleats to the joist. Staggering the joints will increase the strength of the deck and will greatly improve its appearance.

To reduce squeaks and fastener pops, use a deck adhesive as well as spiral or ring-shank nails or deck screws. Use two nails or screws for 4-inch stock, and three for 6-inch boards. Drive the fasteners near the edges of the decking and at a slight angle toward each other. Treated lumber is dense, so it may help to drill it before putting in fasteners. If any wood is splitting, pre-drill it.

KEEP IT STRAIGHT

You won't complete a deck without encountering a warped board or two. Fasten warped boards at one end and work a pry bar

TRIMMING DECK BOARDS

After you've snapped a chalk line, use your circular saw to trim the edges of the decking. Set the saw to just the thickness of the decking.

DECK FASTENERS

Dimples look cute on kids but they detract from a deck's appearance. Hammers create the deck variety—dents made by missing the nail or driving it one time too many.

You can avoid them by fastening your decking with screws. A cordless drill makes the work easy and won't dimple the deck like a hammer and nails will.

Whether you use nails or screws, buy the best: If you're nailing, use ring shank nails. Treated deck screws are better—they hold tighter, last longer, and allow you to remove decking boards more easily and with less damage if the deck needs repairs.

to straighten them and get them in line as you fasten them to each succeeding joist. After each course, measure to the edge of the header and make minor adjustments to keep the final board at full width and parallel. When the decking is complete, snap a chalk line from the edge of the first board to the opposite end. You can also tack a 1×4 to keep the saw straight. Set your circular saw to the depth of the decking and cut along the line.

ALTERNATIVE MATERIALS

Decking doesn't have to be face nailed. Deck connectors are nailed into the sides of the decking to secure it to the joists. Composite decking comes as two-piece, snap-together components or with tongue-and-grooved edges that are blind nailed.

BUILDING A DECK
continued

LAYING OUT A STRINGER

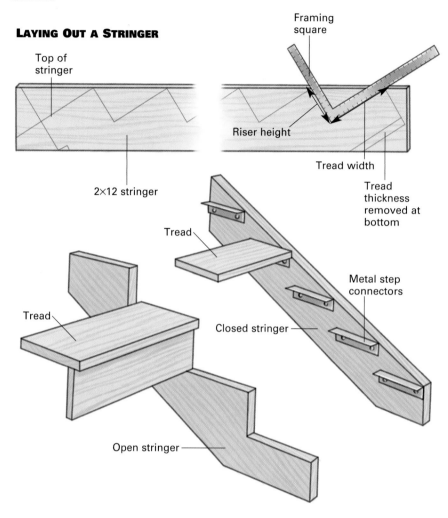

BUILDING STAIRS

Building stairs isn't difficult, but getting them to end at just the right spot does require some preliminary calculations.

DO THE MATH: First, measure the rise of the deck from grade-level to its surface. Divide the total rise by 7 inches—the usual rise between steps. The result is the number of steps you will need.

Next, multiply the number of steps by 11½ inches—the length of a tread made of two 2×6s with a ½-inch gap. This will give you the total run of the stairs—how far from the deck the stairs will end.

Now divide the height of the deck by the number of steps (include the deck surface as a step) to get the actual riser height, which will probably differ from the initial 7-inch estimate.

HOW WIDE? Outdoor stairs need to be at least 36 inches wide. But if you entertain groups, you may want to build them as wide as 5 feet to let two people pass side by side.

LANDING PAD: The base of the stairs should rest on a concrete pad. To build it, mark an area 6 inches wider than your steps and 30 inches from front to back. Excavate it to a depth of 6 inches. Make forms from 2×6s, pour and tamp a 3-inch gravel base, then pour 3 inches of concrete. Insert J-bolts at the locations of your angle iron and let the concrete cure for at least 48 hours.

STRINGERS: The hefty beams that support your steps are called stringers. Your stairs will need a 2×12 stringer on each end and, for stairs wider than 36 inches, a third in the middle. Stringers are either closed or open. Closed stringers are easier to make—you don't have to notch them for the treads. The treads are set between the inside surfaces. Cut the stringers to fit between the deck and concrete pad.

Open stringers will need notches cut for the treads. Mark the riser height on the short end of a carpenter's square and the tread depth on the long side. Fasten short bolts at these measurements. Start with the bottom riser and mark it on the stringer. Moving the square the length of the stringer, mark the "V" cuts for each step, lining up your bolt markers at each line drawn.

Use a circular saw to cut the notches, but stop just short of the point of the cutout and finish it with a handsaw. This way, you'll avoid overcutting. Cut and test fit one stringer, then cut the second to match the first. Use metal joist hangers to attach the stringers to the header and angle iron at the concrete pad.

TREADS AND RISERS: On closed stringers, mark the tread locations and attach the treads with cleats. On an open installation, screw the treads down on the cutouts in the stringer. Attach riser boards behind the treads or leave the spaces open.

RAILING DETAIL

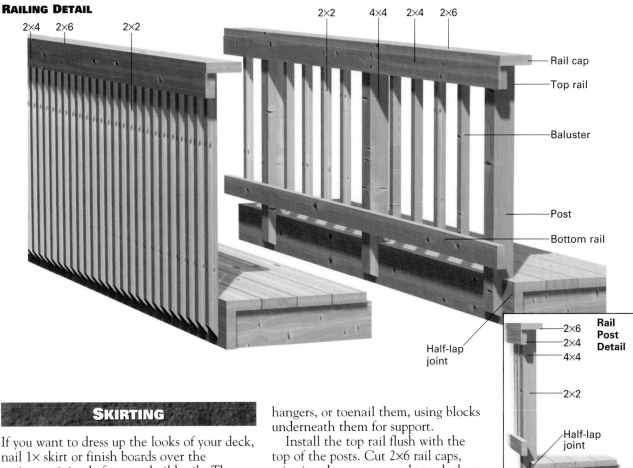

2×4 2×6   2×2

2×2   4×4   2×4   2×6

Rail cap

Top rail

Baluster

Post

Bottom rail

Half-lap joint

Rail Post Detail

2×6
2×4
4×4

2×2

Half-lap joint

SKIRTING

If you want to dress up the looks of your deck, nail 1× skirt or finish boards over the perimeter joists before you build rails. The width of the skirts will depend on the size of the joists and whether the skirts will lie under the edge of the decking or will be flush with the top of the decking boards.

THE RAIL DEAL

Rails can be plain or fancy. So can balusters and spindles. Dimension lumber has a beauty in its own right, or you can cut the stock to match scallops or other vintage trim styles.
HEIGHT: For safety, make the rail at least 36 inches high and space the balusters not more than 4 inches apart to prevent small children from being injured.
PROCESS: Begin at the house and at the corners (if your corner posts are not extended) and attach 4×4 railing posts to the facing at least every 6 feet. Install posts at your stair location, too, cutting their tops to match the angle of descent.

Predrill the posts for washers (offset the holes on the grain), line up the bottom of the posts flush with the bottom of the facing, and drill through the facing and beams.

Fasten the posts with ⅜×7-inch hex bolts. Note that you can surface mount posts on the joists or notch them to fit over the decking.
RAILS: Mark the rail locations on the posts and cut the rail stock so it will fit snugly between them. Attach the railings with rail

hangers, or toenail them, using blocks underneath them for support.

Install the top rail flush with the top of the posts. Cut 2×6 rail caps, mitering the corners, and attach them with 3-inch fasteners.
BALUSTERS: Use prefab balusters or cut your own from 2× stock and attach them with 2½-inch fasteners. Attach them at the bottom first, flush with the bottom of the lower rail, plumb them with a level, and attach the top. Use a 2×4 spacer to keep them uniformly spaced.

FINISHES

Choose deck finishes with care. Paint is not recommended on surfaces subject to foot traffic. Over time, the wear paths show.
CHOICE: Instead, stain or seal your deck. Stain seals and colors the wood. Sealer is clear. Both protect your deck from water damage, and some varieties are mildew- and rot-resistant.

Clean the deck thoroughly before applying either finish, and check the weather forecast first—don't finish your deck if it's going to rain in the next two days.
METHOD: Good old brushing will get the job done. Spraying is faster—certainly more of an adventure—but you will have to mask off the house and other areas to save them from being fogged with stray spray. If your deck is small, use a roller and a brush. They will take more time than spraying but will get the job done.

Most building codes require that railings be added to any deck more than 30 inches above ground, but 30 inches is a long step. Be safer— consider railings or perimeter seating for any deck more than 12 inches above ground. The railing should be at least 36 inches high. To protect small children from injury, space balusters no more than 4 inches apart.

PATIO BASICS

During the planning stage, consider the purpose of the patio, its optimum size, existing doors for patio access, the location of underground utility lines, and whether the patio will be in sun or shade during peak usage. If shade is desired, build an overhead or install a retractable awning that can be adjusted to meet your needs.

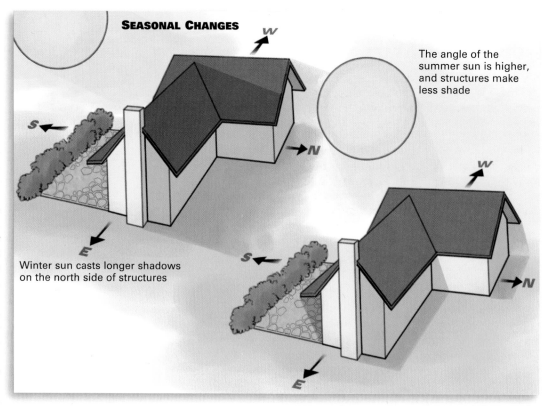

SEASONAL CHANGES

The angle of the summer sun is higher, and structures make less shade

Winter sun casts longer shadows on the north side of structures

Herbert Hoover sought re-election on the promise of "a chicken in every pot." It defined a standard of American life. Today, Hoover might opt instead for "a patio in every backyard."

Patios and decks certainly have become symbols of suburbia. They offer entertainment and seclusion, stretch homes out of doors, and make even towering, vaulted ceilings seem confining in comparison—at a bargain price.

A simple masonry slab is plainly functional, but you can dress it up with aggregate or patterns. Brick and flagstone are even more attractive but also are somewhat more expensive. Planters, masonry walls or benches, and overheads will add a touch of pleasant charm and drama. When choosing materials, let your taste and budget be your guide.

SIZE

To determine the right size for your patio, start with these three considerations:

PROPORTION: One common guideline applies to scale—the area of a patio next to a house should be about a third of the total square footage inside the home. This rule assumes you want a visually pleasing balance of spaces.

COMFORT: Some planners contend that a patio should be at least as large as the room it adjoins. This rule assumes you want a comfortable sense of transition between the house and the patio.

PURPOSE: Your lot, your budget, and your goals will most likely set the scale of your patio. Decide how much space you need for the kind of use you envision, then scale it back to fit the limits of your terrain and finances.

LOCATION

Place your patio to serve its most important function. For example, a patio used primarily for outdoor dining should be close to the kitchen. One intended for recreation might adjoin the game room instead. A patio for sunning and lounging will be most comfortable if built off the master bedroom.

SUN AND SHADE: Take an inventory of your shade and sunshine. Watch how the sun moves across your property at various times of the day during the warm months. Make notes for future reference. The north side of your house may be in almost constant shade, the south side in constant sun. The east will catch the morning sun and the west side, the sunsets. Put stakes in the yard to help keep track of moving shade patterns.

Materials may also affect your comfort and can affect patio microclimates (small areas with their own weather conditions). Masonry slabs make perfect solar collectors and can store enough heat from the afternoon sun to make the evening hours uncomfortable.

You can't make sun, but you can make— or use—shade. If the area is already shaded during the times you'll use the patio, your decisions about location are less complicated. If you need shade, you may need to add an overhead or roll-out awning to your plans.

Try a compromise—a location that is in partial shade and partial sunlight during the hours when patio activity is greatest.

ON THE LEVEL? The ideal patio site will be level so you won't have to contend with costly excavation. If the lawn slopes steeply away from the house, you can fix the slope with a retaining wall and fill with soil. A deck, however, would be less expensive. And remember that when it comes to level ground, perfection isn't required. You'll need to slope the finish ⅛ inch per running foot so water drains away from structures.

OBSTACLES

If you live in a warm climate where snow is not a problem, install your patio so its surface is 1 or 2 inches below floor level. That will keep rain out.

SNOW: In cold climates, the patio should be at least 8 inches below the floor level to keep snow away from the door.

DOORS: If you don't already have access to the patio spot, you can add a door if the patio adjoins a room. And if the access is poorly located, replace it so it serves the traffic flow.

UTILITY LINES: Before making a final decision on patio location, check with utility companies to be sure the patio won't cover buried utility pipes or wires. Some companies will move the lines to avoid access problems in the future.

ENCLOSING A TREE: Patios built around a tree can appear as if nature put them there, but take care to avoid damage to the root system. If a tree will be the life of your patio, don't let your patio be the death of the tree. Construction machinery can crush and tear roots, and a concrete slab can starve a tree

of water and nutrients. Remember, the major root system of a tree is as broad as its branches. Those roots need to have access to water. Brick-in-sand or dry-laid flagstones permit rain to enter and reach the roots. Build an edging of 6×6 timbers around the tree base, well away from exposed tree roots. Secure the timbers with 2-foot rebar.

MICROCLIMATES

Cool air (top left) is drawn down into the patio. The wall and patio (lower left) absorb daytime heat; stored heat (above) is released at night.

ALTERNATIVE MATERIALS

Pavers Flagstone Decking Gravel

The choices of patio materials are almost infinite. Concrete can be topped with exposed aggregate, stamped with a special tool that simulates a brick or stone pattern, or can have coloring added before the pour. In climates where frost heave is a problem, install permanent wood or masonry edging, then dry-lay brick, pavers, or flagstone over a base of gravel and sand. Sweep the surface with sand to fill the cracks and stabilize the brick or stones.

For a patio of brick or stone in mortar you must pour and tamp a 4-inch gravel base, then pour a 4-inch concrete pad. When the concrete is set, lay a bed of mortar on the pad and embed the brick or stones. Let the mortar cure, then grout the joints with mortar.

PATIO BASICS
continued

PATIO SITE PREPARATION

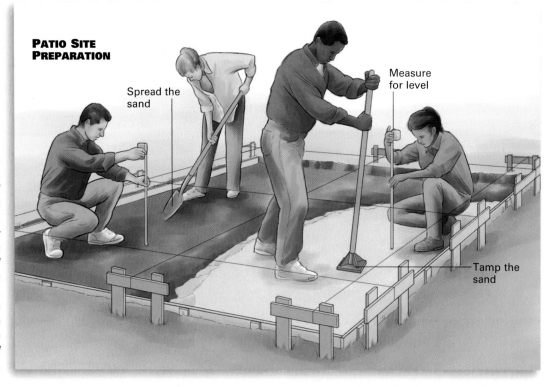

Spread the sand

Measure for level

Tamp the sand

To prepare the patio site, measure and mark the perimeter, setting batter boards so lines are square and intersect at the patio corners. Excavate the area and place and tamp the gravel or sand base.

LAYOUT

Prepare for patio excavation by measuring the dimensions and marking the corners with temporary stakes. Set up batter boards just beyond the corners (see page 70 for more information) and attach mason's lines to the crossbars.

SQUARE: The simple "3-4-5 test" will tell you if corners are square. Don't graduate to the next step until you pass this test.

From the corner, measure out 3 feet on one line and mark the spot with tape. Measure 4 feet from the corner along the other side and mark that point. Adjust the mason's line until the diagonal distance between the marks is exactly 5 feet.

MARK POSTS: Drop a plumb bob from the intersection of the mason's lines and move your stakes to these points. Tie line tautly from stake to stake and mark the patio outline on the ground with chalk or spray paint.

DO IT YOURSELF OR CONTRACT IT?

Should you do the excavation work yourself or hire it done? The answer will depend on the size of the excavation, materials, and the amount of earth to be moved.

If soil must be taken from the site, the contracting costs for the excavation and soil removal may offset your expenses for hauling and dumping.

EXCAVATING

The depth of the excavation will be the sum of all its components. Here's a guide to excavation depths for various materials:

BRICK OR STONE IN SAND: 8 to 9 inches (4 inches of gravel base, 2 inches of sand, and 2 to 3 inches of brick or stone). Brick- or stone-in-sand construction does not require a solid foundation. These materials are intended to heave with the earth in freezing weather and return to level when the frost is out of the ground. It is the moisture in the ground that expands when freezing, and the thick gravel base minimizes the heaving.

POURED CONCRETE: 8 inches (4-inch gravel base and 4 inches of concrete).

MORTARED BRICK OR STONE: 10½ to 12 inches (8 inches of gravel and concrete base, ½- to 1-inch mortar bed, and 2 to 3 inches of brick or stone).

Remember that the surface of the patio should be about an inch above grade level to permit rain to flow off the patio. So subtract that amount from the depths, and your patio surface will be slightly above soil level. A patio raised by this amount will also allow you to mow the edges without having to trim them separately.

In cold climates, some local codes require slabs for poured concrete and mortared patios to "float"—to permit the slab to heave in one piece. Excavate a trench a foot beyond the patio perimeter and 6 inches deeper than the

SCREEDING THE SAND

Forms or permanent edging

Screed

Leveled sand base

PLYWOOD FOR CURVED FORMS

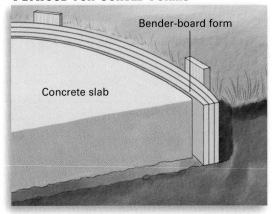

Bender-board form

Concrete slab

BRICK IN SAND

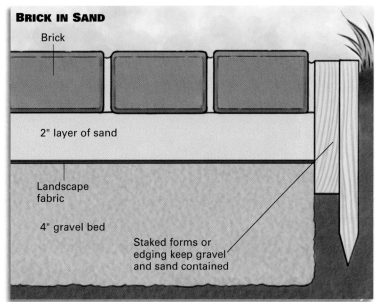

Brick

2" layer of sand

Landscape fabric

4" gravel bed

Staked forms or edging keep gravel and sand contained

CONCRETE SLAB

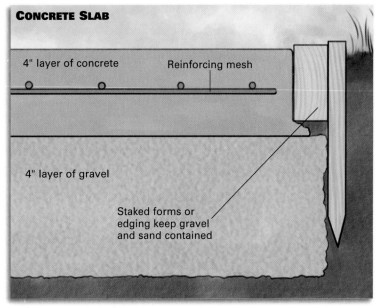

4" layer of concrete

Reinforcing mesh

4" layer of gravel

Staked forms or edging keep gravel and sand contained

BRICK IN CONCRETE

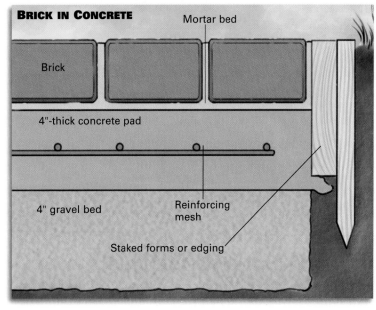

Mortar bed

Brick

4"-thick concrete pad

4" gravel bed

Reinforcing mesh

Staked forms or edging

---

patio excavation. You'll need to lay a gravel base in the trench the same depth as the footing. Dig out the turf about 6 inches beyond the lines to allow for forms.

FORMS OR EDGING

When finished digging, build forms for any project that calls for concrete, or install any edging you plan to use. Stakes will secure permanent edging or concrete forms in place.

Set the forms so the slab slopes for drainage at a rate of ⅛ inch per running foot.

Drop the mason's line to the final grade of the patio and lay in your paver or timber edging, or the forms for concrete.

SCREED: You can make your own screed—the straight-edge tool you'll use to level loose material. You'll need a 2×4 long enough to span the forms and some ⅜-inch plywood, long enough to fit edge-to-edge between your forms. Attach the plywood to the 2×4 so that, when the 2×4 rests across the forms, the plywood defines the depth of the bed. After you've leveled the bed with a rake, drag the screed across the bedding material. Screeds work better with two people, one at one end and one at the other. Screeds also work better when you work them across the forms in a back-and-forth sawing motion.

CONCRETE AND MORTAR PATIOS

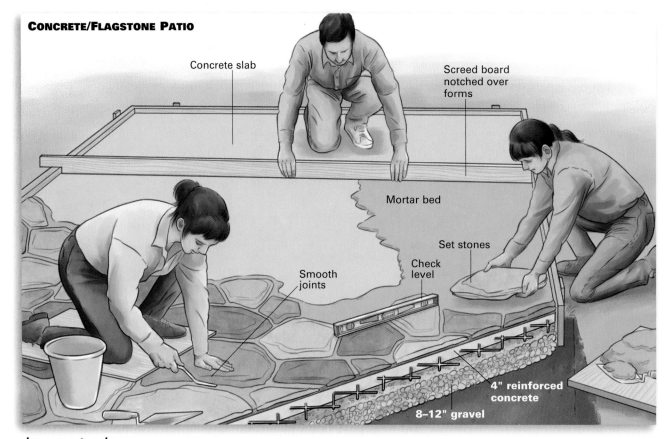

CONCRETE/FLAGSTONE PATIO

Concrete slab

Screed board notched over forms

Mortar bed

Smooth joints

Set stones

Check level

4" reinforced concrete

8–12" gravel

Lay a mortared flagstone patio directly over a concrete slab (supported by a gravel bed). You can level the mortar with a screed, but don't lay too much mortar at once— it sets up quickly. After the stones have been set, wait 24 hours before filling and tooling the joints.

POURED CONCRETE

Building a concrete patio is a lot like building walls, except you're working on a larger scale. First, lay out and excavate the site.

MAKING FORMS: Drive 2×4 stakes slightly behind your corner markers, and build the forms with 2×8s, nailing them to the stakes and to each other with duplex nails. Splice joints with ½-inch plywood.

GRAVEL BED: Next lay a gravel bed in the excavation. Level it roughly with a garden rake and then with a screed (*see page 79*). Once it's level, tamp it with a rented tamper.

REINFORCING WIRE: Lay 6×6 number 10 reinforcing wire mesh on bricks to keep it centered vertically in the poured slab. Tie overlapping sections with wire and tie the mesh to the bricks also.

MIX AND POUR: If your site is small, you can mix the concrete yourself. Large sites will need ready mix delivered. Consolidate the pour with a shovel; use a 2×4 to level it.

FINISH: Give the wet surface a brick or stone pattern with a stamping tool, or trowel it smooth. For an aggregate finish, spread small smooth stone over the surface. Work it in with a bull float. After the concrete begins to set, spray it with water until the stones show.

MORTARED MASONRY

By now, you have excavated to a depth equal to the combined thickness of the materials. Follow the steps for poured concrete (*left*). You are actually making a base patio underground. Let the concrete set for three to seven days.

PATTERNS: Brick patios are usually laid in running bond, common bond, or herringbone patterns. If you choose a pattern that will require much cutting, rent a water-cooled masonry saw.

Stone sizes, shapes, and thickness vary, so lay them in a random pattern on the ground next to your curing concrete. Use small stones to fill the gaps between irregularly shaped stones. Take your time and experiment until you get a pattern you want. When you are ready to lay the stones in the patio, move them in sequence from the lawn to reproduce your test pattern.

MORTAR: When the concrete pad is cured, lay a mortar base (½ inch for brick, an inch for stone). Spread only small areas at a time— mortar sets up quickly. You don't want to try to chip off mistakes. When the mortar has set for 24 hours, use a mortar bag to grout the cracks, and smooth them with a jointing tool.

BRICKS AND STONES IN SAND

A brick-in-sand patio must have permanent edgings to hold the materials in place. Stone does not.

EDGING: Excavate to the proper depth, then install the edging. Brick and timber are good choices, and timber makes attractive divisions if you build in sections.

GRAVEL BASE: Inside the edgings, pour in a 4-inch gravel base. Level it with a garden rake and screed, and tamp it firmly.

LANDSCAPE FABRIC: Lay landscape fabric over the gravel to control vegetation growth. Overlap joints at least 8 inches.

SAND: Put in a 2-inch layer of sand and level it. Wet the area to settle the sand, then tamp it to ensure that the base will not settle after you have laid the bricks or stones.

LAY THE SURFACE: To ensure alignment and uniform joints for brick, use spacers or a mason's line as a guide. Check the level of the bricks or stones frequently.

SWEEP: After laying the entire surface, sweep mason's sand in the cracks to lock the bricks or stones into position. When the patio is done, wet the sand joints with a fine mist to pack the sand tight, and again sweep with sand to ensure that the joints are filled.

PATIO DRAINAGE

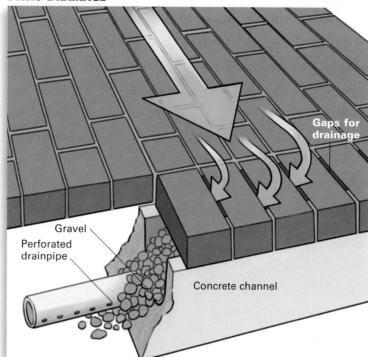

Gravel
Perforated drainpipe
Gaps for drainage
Concrete channel

Gaps in the mortar joints allow water to run into the concrete channel and drainpipe for dispersal to a drain field or storm drain.

Begin a brick-in-sand patio by laying landscape fabric beneath the sand. Wet and tamp the sand to prevent settling. If bricks are not level, remove them and add sand to return them to level.

BRICK IN SAND

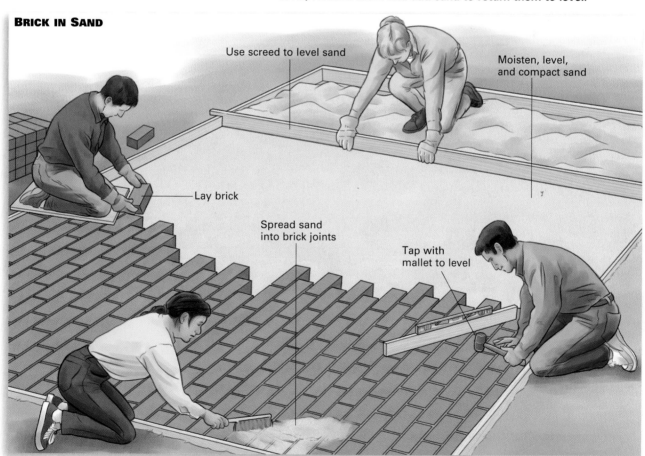

Use screed to level sand

Moisten, level, and compact sand

Lay brick

Spread sand into brick joints

Tap with mallet to level

MADE IN THE SHADE: OVERHEADS

An overhead can be airy and open, as above, or partially or fully enclosed with a wood or canvas roof and lattice or other screening for the walls. The posts should be set with one-third of their length into the ground or firmly anchored to deck posts so they'll hold up to the wind and support the weight of the overhead. Benches provide a pleasant spot for relaxation or reading. Add seat backs for more comfort.

You may be one of those impatient souls who simply cannot wait for a shade tree to grow from the sapling you planted last year. You want relief from the searing summer sun? And you want it *now*? Shade structures can sprout in a weekend and serve your needs for years—maybe even until that tree grows up.

Build an overhead to shelter a deck, or include seating in an isolated overhead shelter to create a retreat for reading, conversation, or contemplation. Here are some general principles:

POSTS FOR DECKS: All overheads start with posts. If you've extended your posts above your decking (to the right height), your post-setting is already done. If you're adding an overhead to an existing deck, install the posts directly over the deck posts. Use ½-inch bolts with washers and brace them to prevent movement.

POSTS FOR PATIOS: To shade a patio, first install piers (see "Setting Deck Posts," page 70). Posts will shrink slightly as they age, leaving space in concrete settings, so caulk the base of the posts after the concrete cures.

On a patio with a finished concrete pad, drill holes in the concrete at the center of

the posts and attach a post base to the slab.

Space the posts no more than 12 feet apart and, if you're digging, at a depth equal to one-third their length (a 12-foot post would be set 4 feet in the ground). Set posts deeper than the local frost depth. A heavy, shingled roof will need 6×6 posts or 4×4s set no more than 6 feet apart.

FRAMING: To attach an overhead to your house, fasten a ledger board high enough for headroom (its bottom edge at least 7½ feet high). Predrill and attach the ledger into studs in the wall with ½-inch lag screws.

If you want to carve decorative patterns or trim lines into your beams, do it now— before installation.

Next, fasten the beams to the posts and suspend the joists in joist hangers. Use metal connectors to fasten the posts and rafters to beams, and hurricane ties to secure the wooden cross members to the joists.

Frame-building for an overhead follows the same general procedure as deck building (*see sections beginning on page 66*).

Finally add a canopy, such as a grid of 2× stock, wood or vinyl lattice, an open design of your choice, or a shed rooftop.

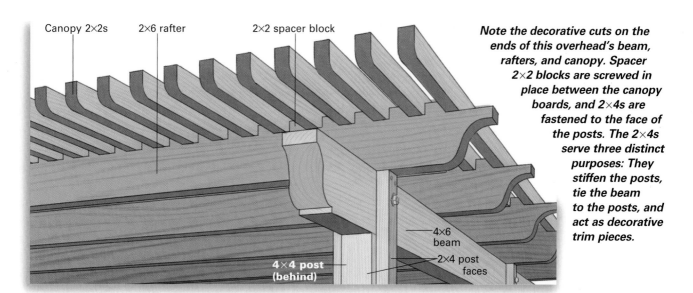

Canopy 2×2s 2×6 rafter 2×2 spacer block 4×6 beam 4×4 post (behind) 2×4 post faces

Note the decorative cuts on the ends of this overhead's beam, rafters, and canopy. Spacer 2×2 blocks are screwed in place between the canopy boards, and 2×4s are fastened to the face of the posts. The 2×4s serve three distinct purposes: They stiffen the posts, tie the beam to the posts, and act as decorative trim pieces.

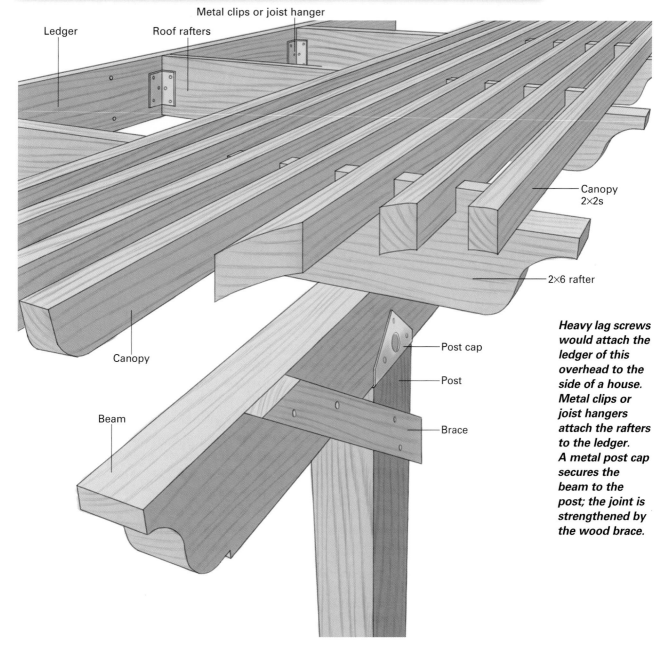

Metal clips or joist hanger Ledger Roof rafters Canopy 2×2s 2×6 rafter Canopy Post cap Post Beam Brace

Heavy lag screws would attach the ledger of this overhead to the side of a house. Metal clips or joist hangers attach the rafters to the ledger. A metal post cap secures the beam to the post; the joint is strengthened by the wood brace.

GENTLE GAZEBOS

This Victorian-style gazebo, modeled after the classic designs of that period, makes an attractive backyard getaway. The style and construction offer a number of design alternative as described in this section.

Whether they're built with four, six, or eight sides, gazebos brighten any landscape. The "dark side" is those angles can pose a complicated geometry puzzle.

One solution can be bought: Garden and building centers sell precut gazebo kits. The kits come with all pieces cut to size and angle. They're even numbered for easy assembly.

ONE STEP AT A TIME

If you're patient and careful, you can have the satisfaction of building your own gazebo. Designs can be found in garden magazines, if you seek inspiration.

MATERIALS: The Victorian-style eight-sided gazebo above uses 6×6 posts and 3×6 rafters from each post to the rooftop hub.

The width of 3×6s will let the rafters meet at the hub, yet is wide enough to hold the nails and the roof decking. Your lumberyard may not stock this material but should be able to order it for you.

You will need seven 8-foot and one 10-foot 6×6s, and sufficient 3×6s for eight sides.

SHAPE THE POSTS: To shape the 6×6 posts, set the blade on your circular saw at a 45-degree angle and cut each corner along the length of the eight beams. Use a rip guide to keep your cutting straight. On rip-cuts of this length, your blade must be sharp. The saw is set for its maximum cutting depth and will be working at full capacity. If it bogs down, decrease its cutting depth and make more than one pass.

Now you've made octagonal posts with 2¼-inch-wide faces. Remove the saw marks with a belt sander or power planer, but do so with care—both tools remove wood quickly. Next cut 2 feet off the 10-foot 6×6. You will use the shorter piece for the roof hub.

FOUNDATIONS: You can build your gazebo on a concrete pad or patio, or over a deck. To lay out its shape, start with a 12-foot square and follow the diagram on page 86 to plot and mark the post locations. On concrete, mark the centers of the posts, drill, and install concrete anchors. Otherwise, dig postholes to the frost line and use concrete form tubes to pour piers (see "Setting Deck Posts" page 70). On any installation, use a template traced from the bottom of one of the posts to mark the exact placement of the post facings. Mount the posts on the foundation or piers with post connectors. On any surface, brace all the posts with 1×4s before framing.

PERSPECTIVE VIEW

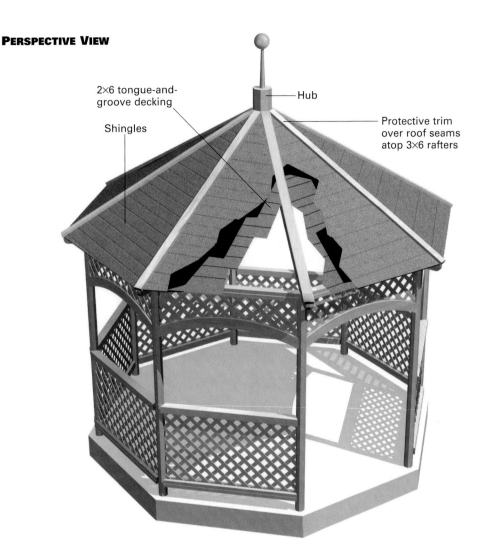

2×6 tongue-and-groove decking

Hub

Shingles

Protective trim over roof seams atop 3×6 rafters

This gazebo design will adapt to a number of different wall and archway materials.

The roof framing of this octagonal gazebo consists of just eight 3×6 rafters, secured to the top wall plates and to a center hub (see page 86) at the peak. Because the span between posts is 54 inches, you must use 2×6 tongue-and-groove decking, rather than plywood, for roof sheathing. If you're plagued by insects, screen the open areas and add a screen door.

DECORATIVE TOUCHES FOR YOUR GAZEBO

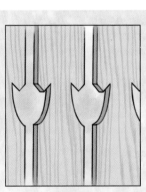

To add decorative touches to your gazebo, scroll-cut rafter ends (*below*). ■ To emphasize the roof, use wood-tone asphalt shingles, cedar shingles, or hand-split shakes. ■ Top the roof hub post with a finial or a weather vane, or alter the roof design to include jack rafters and headers, then build a cupola to crown the gazebo and provide roof ventilation. ■ Replace the plywood arches shown *opposite* with scroll-sawn brackets cut in an interesting pattern. Check your building-supply center for precut scrolled brackets. ■ Cut scroll patterns on rails and balusters. ■ Substitute round or narrow balusters or lattice for the 1×8 balusters shown. ■ Or for more privacy, cover some or all of the wall sections completely with lattice, from top to bottom.

Scroll-cut rafter

■ If you build a gazebo on a concrete slab, consider building a walk of mortared brick or flagstone to the door, then continue the brick or flagstone finish on the gazebo floor. ■ Or use a stamping tool to create a brick or stone pattern in the poured concrete. ■ If you live in mosquito country, build screen panels and install them between the posts, and add a screen door. ■ If the gazebo is built over a wood deck, install aluminum screening over the deck joists in the gazebo area. This will prevent mosquitoes or other insects from entering through the cracks between deck boards. ■ For hot summer weather, run electrical wiring to the roof hub post and install a ceiling fan with lights. ■ Electrical outlets installed on the posts can provide power for a fan, radio, TV, or appliances such as coffee pots or skillets.

GENTLE GAZEBOES
continued

PLAN VIEW

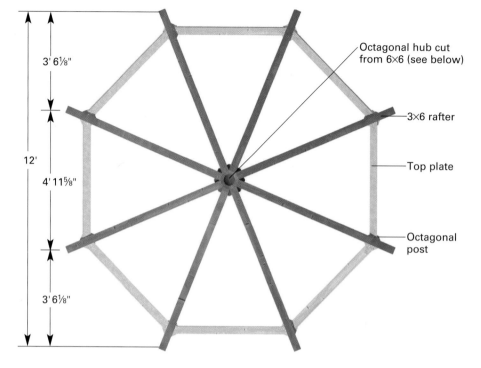

3' 6⅛"

12'

4' 11⅝"

3' 6⅛"

Octagonal hub cut from 6×6 (see below)

3×6 rafter

Top plate

Octagonal post

POST/HUB DETAIL

Use a circular or table saw set to 45°. Cut the corners of each 6×6 post to form an octagon. Position the posts so that the arches and railings will fit flat against the faces of the posts.

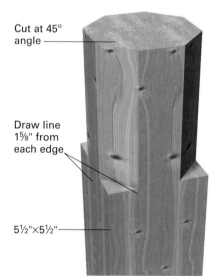

Cut at 45° angle

Draw line 1⅝" from each edge

5½"×5½"

FINISHING THE GAZEBO

It's best to seal the cut ends of gazebo components or even paint or stain completely before assembling the gazebo. The traditional Victorian-style gazebo was painted white, but you may want to paint or stain it to match your house or to match other outdoor structures such as a privacy fence or deck. A handheld spray gun will speed staining or painting.

FRAMING: Check the posts for level with a line level and cut the first to 7 feet 8 inches, adjusting the remaining posts if necessary and checking with a water level. Then cut the top plates to 22½-degree angles. Attach short bolts to your framing square at 5 inches on the tongue (the short side) and 12 inches on the blade (the long side). Align the bolted marks on the edge of each top plate, then mark and cut the angle.

If you plan to install inset arches, cut grooves in the posts and top plates before attaching them with 16d nails. For added strength, use metal connectors and tie corners together with plate straps.

Next install the arches made of curved braces laminated to ½-inch ABX plywood and set in grooves in the posts and top plates. Arches are not only decorative; they also tie the posts together in one consistent unit.

MAKING RAFTERS: Follow the diagram (*opposite*) to cut the rafters. Cut one rafter according to the diagram, test fit it, and use it as a form to mark the others.

The tail of the rafters can be rounded as a decorative touch. (Of course, you can cut the rafter tail straight or substitute your own decorative pattern for the one shown.)

Cut the bird's mouth, which fits the end of the rafter over the top plate, 10½ inches from the tail of the rafter.

Cut the roof hub from the 24-inch 6×6 cut earlier. The roof hub should be 16 inches long and set at the center of the roof; the 3×6 rafters will bear against it on the eight sides.

Because the rafter width is slightly more than the width of the post faces, you'll have to bevel their ends with a block plane. The hub extends above the shingles on the finished roof; position the rafter ends against the hub so that several inches of the hub are exposed on the roof.

SETTING RAFTERS: From this point you will need at least one helper and assembled scaffolding to set the rafters. Use a screw gun and 4-inch screws to attach two opposing rafters to the center hub.

Predrill the holes and soap the screws to keep from splitting the wood. Then turn the paired assembly right-side-up and set the rafters on top of the wall plates with the bird's mouths centered on the posts.

Toenail the paired rafters to the top plate, then position and secure the other rafters.

ROOF DECKING: With all the rafters positioned and secured, cut and nail the 2×6 tongue-and-groove decking over the rafters to sheath the roof.

Because the top of the decking will be covered with shingles and the bottom side exposed as ceiling, put the best side down. Use 10d galvanized nails to secure the decking to the rafters.

If you find it difficult to cut the decking to match the angles of the rafters, run the boards past the rafters, then center a chalk-line down the sheathing over the center line of the rafters. Set your circular saw to the sheathing depth and cut the sheathing. If you use this gang-cut method, drive only enough nails to hold the boards in place, and position nails in the rafters so the saw blade will not hit them when cutting.

Shingle the roof as desired. Cedar shingles or hand-split shakes make an attractive addition to the gazebo. Asphalt shingles can match those on the house roof. Attach a finial or weather vane to the top of the hub.

RAILINGS: You can build railings on seven sides, as shown in the illustrations. Notch the posts to a ⅝-inch depth with a circular saw to accommodate the top rails, and install paneling or balusters.

To set the angle at the top of the rafters—where they meet the peak's center post—use a framing square. Lay the square over the rafter so that the scale on the side nearest the roof peak reads 8 and the scale along the rooftop surface reads 12.

RAFTER CONSTRUCTION

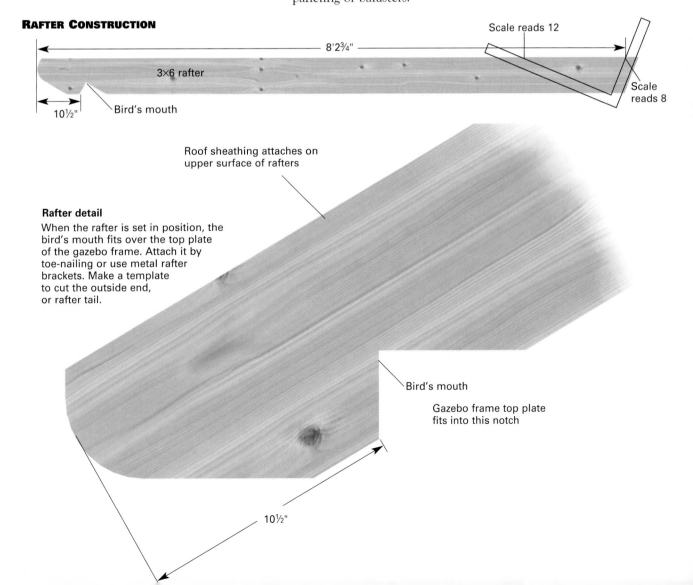

Scale reads 12

8'2¾"

3×6 rafter

Bird's mouth

10½"

Scale reads 8

Roof sheathing attaches on upper surface of rafters

Rafter detail
When the rafter is set in position, the bird's mouth fits over the top plate of the gazebo frame. Attach it by toe-nailing or use metal rafter brackets. Make a template to cut the outside end, or rafter tail.

Bird's mouth

Gazebo frame top plate fits into this notch

10½"

SHEDS

This inexpensive shed is easy to build. Use 2×8 floor joists and 2×6 rafters for spans up to 12 feet. Build a ramp of treated wood so you can roll lawn equipment in and out of the shed. The window is optional; you'll want the daylight in a workshop shed, but it's not needed for space that's strictly for storage.

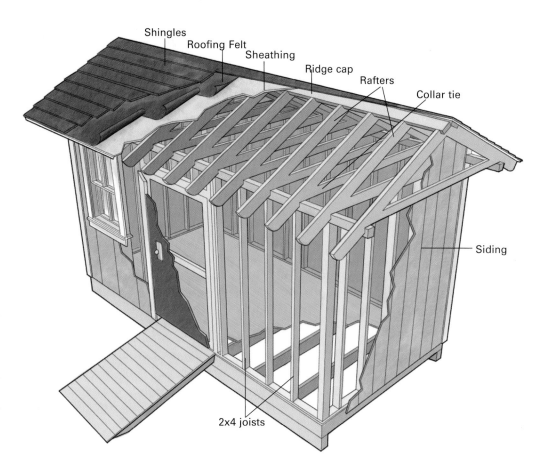

Shingles
Roofing Felt
Sheathing
Ridge cap
Rafters
Collar tie
Siding
2x4 joists

If your garage is so jammed with tools, toys, and bikes that your car has to park outside, it's time to build a storage shed—or to have a sale.

Better organization might solve some of your problems—shelves and hooks can unclutter the floor and neatly stash a truckload of treasures. But you'll need added space for large or bulky items such as bags of fertilizer, lawnmowers, or garden tractors.

SOLUTIONS IN STORE

WEATHER VANE CUPOLA CROWN

A storage shed provides an easy solution—and might put off that nasty garage-sale option for years.

STYLISH STORAGE: The design and finish of your storage shed can match the design of your house or of other outbuildings. A shed can resemble a small-scale gambrel-roofed barn, or can have a modern look, sided in redwood lap or plywood panels. Even prefab sheds can be decorative. Vine-covered trellises can make them seem as if they're growing out of the landscape. Paint can help make them fade away.

HOW BIG? If you need a storage shed only to relieve a garage clutter of rakes and hockey sticks, build a simple lean-to along your house or garage wall. Sheds can be as small as a closet, but if you need space for garden tractors and lawn-care equipment, you may want something the size of a small garage.

CUSTOMIZING: The features you include in a shed depend on its purpose.

■ **GARDENING:** A gardener may want a potting shed with shelves for flower pots and watering cans, and a bench to pot plants on. Include a bench on rollers or provide room for roll-out bins for fertilizer and potting soil.

■ **WORKSHOP:** If the shed will be your workshop, include a workbench large enough to hold your power tools. Put pegboard on the walls for hand tools. You'll want electric service to the shed to power the tools, and a bench light for good visibility. Unlike simple storage sheds, workshops need windows. Equip all electrical outlets with ground fault circuit interrupters to prevent shocks.

PREFAB OPTIONS: Aluminum or painted-steel shed kits require very little labor. Most of them are held together by sheet-metal screws or by nuts and bolts and come with assembly instructions. A power screwdriver or nut driver makes assembly of these sheds an easy weekend project. You'll find wood-kit options, too. Their assembly is a relatively simple hammer-and-nail process.

BUILDING YOUR OWN

If you're going to build your own shed, save time with simplicity. Build a concrete slab for floor and foundation, or a wooden floor on skids or concrete piers. Use 2× stock for framing, and sheath the floor, walls, and roof with exterior-grade plywood.

To start your project, select a level area. Put a gambrel-roofed and stylish shed in a prominent location as a focal point. For the strictly functional, choose a remote corner.

Outline your site with rope and move in the lawn equipment and other items within the roped perimeters. Adjust the space so you can get to everything easily. The general rule for storage sheds is there is never enough room, so plan a generous size and then add 2 feet to each dimension.

FOUNDATIONS: A poured concrete pad is strong, easy to build, and durable. Concrete cleans easily if you seal the floors. A skid floor requires less excavation.

■ **CONCRETE PAD:** Setting concrete for a large shed requires the same excavation and preparation you would use for a concrete walk

PIER FOUNDATION

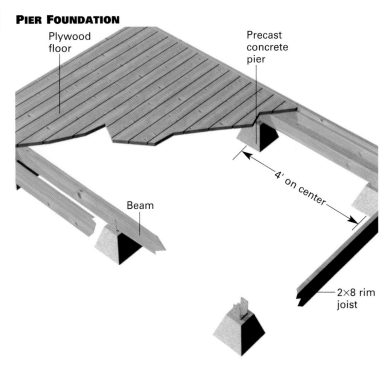

Plywood floor

Precast concrete pier

Beam

4' on center

2×8 rim joist

RAFTER DIAGRAM

Overhang

3½"

2×6 rafter stock

Ridge cut mark

Bird's mouth

12"

6"

Rafter plus overhang

GABLE SHED ROOF

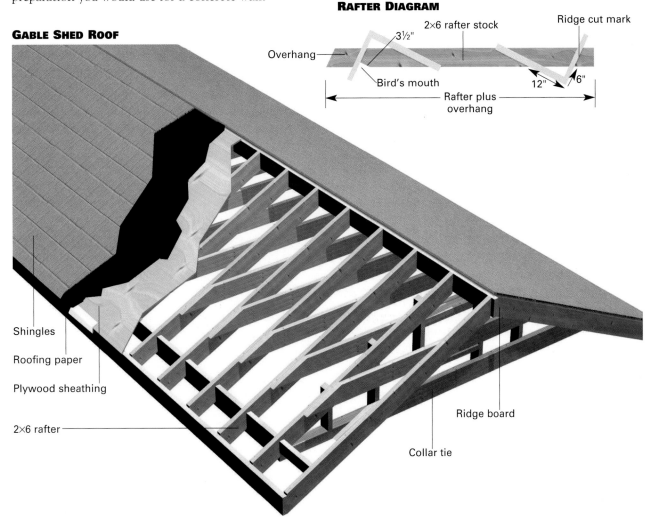

Shingles

Roofing paper

Plywood sheathing

2×6 rafter

Ridge board

Collar tie

SHEDS
continued

PREHUNG DOOR

When framing a door opening, leave a gap of at least ⅜ inch on each side and top to adjust and plumb the precut door in the opening. Plumb the door in the opening and use wood shims at corners, hinge, and lock locations. Nail through the door frame at shim locations and through the molding around the door.

or patio. Excavate, form, and pour the concrete pad according to the steps for patios on pages 78 to 80.

Small sheds won't be affected by frost heave, so you can use precast concrete piers set on 6-inch poured concrete pads. Insert treated 4×4 posts into the precast piers and level them 8 inches above the ground. This height will keep the floor high and dry in rainy weather and hold the beams above the snow level in most areas.

Cut rim and floor joists from 2×8s, and set the floor joists 16 inches on center with blocking for additional strength. Sheds less than 12 feet wide won't need the blocking. Next lay treated or exterior ¾-inch plywood for the floor, securing it with 8d spiral flooring nails or screws spaced about 8 inches apart.

■ **WOODEN SKIDS:** You won't have to excavate as deeply for a skid floor,

but you will still need to dig for a 6-inch gravel base. Remove the sod from your outlined area, and dig the foundation. Pour gravel, then level and tamp it.

Next, install the skids—tripled, pressure-treated 2×8s, nailed together with 16d galvanized nails.

Miter the skids at their bottom corners and anchor them with metal connectors to 2-foot number-4 rebar, driven into the ground. You can pull the rebar anchors to move the shed whenever you decide it needs a change of scene.

WALLS AND DOORS: Use treated 2×4s for the bottom—the sole plates—of the walls, cut in multiples of 24 inches. Walls and roof rafters can be framed 24 inches on center. For sheds up to 12 feet wide use 2×4 collar beams below the ridge board to tie opposing rafters together.

The illustration (*left*) shows a standard-width house door. If you will store power lawn equipment such as a lawnmower or tractor, you will need a wider door, and you will have to build the frame yourself. Make it double wide with 2-foot doors hung in a 4-foot opening. Build the doors of ¾-inch treated plywood, framed with 1×4s nailed to all four edges. Use two or three heavy-duty galvanized strap hinges to support the jamb edge of each door, and add a heavy-duty hasp and padlock.

INTERIOR: Leave the interior of the shed unfinished: The bare wall studs make shelf-building simple. Metal hangers are also handy for storing items off the floor.

Because painted floors will show wear patterns, do not paint the floor. Use a clear wood sealer to prevent spilled liquids from staining it.

DOUBLE DOORS

To provide wider door access for storing yard equipment, install double doors on your yard shed. Build the doors using ½-inch exterior plywood, with 1×4 edging, cross brace, and trim. Use heavy-duty exterior-grade hinges to support the door.

BUILDING A LEAN-TO SHED

If you need only a small shed to eliminate garage clutter, a lean-to may be the answer to your storage problems. You can build a lean-to shed against any existing house or garage wall. Most are the size of a closet, usually 2×4 feet, but they can be as large as 4×8 feet.

LOCATIONS

A lean-to shed built on a deck is simple to construct. Deck locations eliminate the need for flooring and foundation work and make the job easy. Leans-tos built on soil will need a foundation—either of concrete or gravel. For a concrete pad, excavate the soil to a depth of 8 inches. Fill the excavation with 4 inches of gravel for drainage. Then form and pour a 4-inch concrete floor. Insert 4-inch foundation bolts up to their threads in the wet concrete, and after the concrete is cured, attach treated-lumber 2×4 sill plates. On existing concrete pads, use a masonry drill and self-drilling masonry anchors to attach the bolts for sill plates.

If you build the shed on a wood deck, use galvanized 10d nails to anchor the sole plates to the decking. Frame the walls of the shed as shown in the illustration (right), starting with a leveled ledger. Use exterior screws of suitable length to attach the corner 2×4s to the wall. The length of the screws depends on the thickness and type of siding on the house. The screws must penetrate through the 2×4, the siding and sheathing, and 2 inches into the wall studs.

DOORWAYS

Door-width is critical for maximum accessibility. Stock house doors are usually no more than 3 feet wide, so the best alternative is to build wider double doors of ¾-inch plywood framed with 1×4s. The pair of narrow doors require less room to swing than a single-wide door. Frame the door opening in the front wall of the shed, using a doubled 2×6 for the header.

STUDS AND RAFTERS

When the wall studs are in place, attach a second top plate. This 2×4 top plate must overlap the adjoining top plates at the corners of the wall. Use 10d galvanized nails to attach it.

Attach the 2×4 rafters to the ledger with joist hangers, and use 10d galvanized nails to secure the rafters to the wall top plate. Cover the roof with ½-inch plywood, felt roofing paper, and shingles. Install aluminum flashing between the wall siding and the roof. Flashing keeps rainwater from collecting behind and under the roofing materials.

The roof flashing must extend under the joint in the siding and over the shingles. Seal with roof mastic.

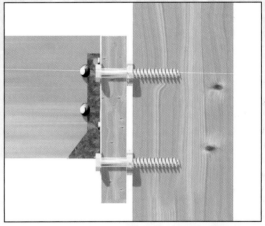

Position washers or shims behind the ledger to plumb the ledger face on the beveled siding.

Make plywood doors of ½-inch plywood framed with 1×4s.

1×4   ½ plywood

GARDEN BEDS

Raised and framed by wooden timbers, garden beds offer many advantages to the gardener. They eliminate damage to flowers from lawn mowers, provide straight and built-in edging to keep grass or weeds from encroaching, and give you a place to build your garden soil to order.

MATERIALS: Use cedar, redwood, or pressure-treated lumber for your edging—2×10s, multiple 2×6s, or stacked 4×4s. Although these woods are durable and rot-resistant, you should apply a coat of clear wood sealer to the surfaces of all the wood components before you assemble them.

COMFORT BONUS: If you attach 2×10 seats on the frame walls, you'll thank yourself every time you don't have to stoop or kneel to tend your plantings.

A raised bed has advantages for the plants and for the gardener. Fill the bed with black dirt, humus, or compost and improve garden soil quality by simply covering over the existing soil. The 2×10 perimeter seat allows you to tend the garden while seated.

DIVING IN

Choose a level site or a slope that won't require much leveling. Lay out the perimeter with mason's lines and batter boards.

CHECK SQUARE: Mark one line with tape 3 feet from the intersection and another at 4 feet. When the distance between the marks is 5 feet, the corners are square.

BOBBING FOR POSTS: Drop a plumb bob at the corners and drive in stakes. Tie a line between the stakes and mark the bed perimeter with chalk or spray paint.

Remove the sod and save it for low or bare spots in the yard. Loosen the soil with a roto tiller, then dig a trench 3 to 4 inches deep.

INSTALL THE EDGING

If you're using 2× stock, dig 3-foot holes and install 4×4 posts as corner anchors and at midpoints on long spans. Cut them level at the height of your edging, using a mason's line as a guide. Stacked timbers will not need corner or midpoint posts.

Attach 2× stock to the posts with lag screws or carriage bolts, or lay in the timbers with overlapping joints. Drill timbers and drive rerod into the soil. For either stock, extend the top piece to make a brace for seating. Seating will also require braces at 6-foot intervals. Use 2×10s for seats and fasten with carriage bolts.

Cover the planting area with landscape fabric to control weed growth. Then, add the soil mixture that best fits the needs of your plantings.

RAISED GARDEN BED

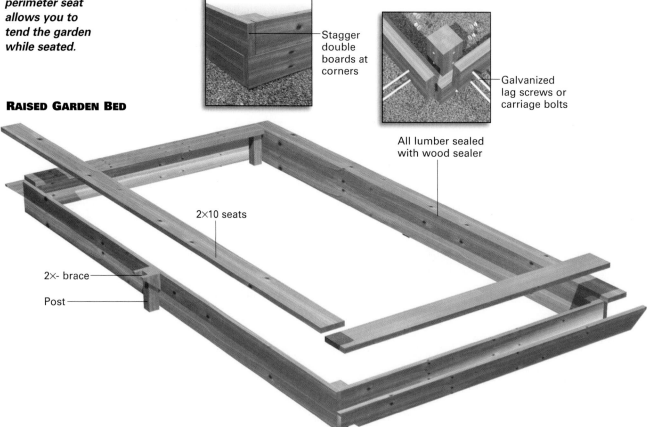

Stagger double boards at corners

Galvanized lag screws or carriage bolts

All lumber sealed with wood sealer

2×10 seats

2×- brace

Post

COMPOST BINS

Compost bins make waste disposal easy, and compost is a valuable addition to the soil in garden beds. Spread the compost as a top dressing on the lawn, till it into garden soil, or mix it with equal parts of perlite and sand or loam to make your own potting soil.

Because it takes weeks to reduce waste to compost, build three bins—one for fresh discards, a second for cooking, and a third for finished compost.

LOCATION: Choose your bin location carefully. Even well-managed compost bins generate odors, so place them—and manage them—so the odors do not offend the neighbors.

DIMENSIONS: Each bin illustrated below is 3 feet high, 3 feet wide, and 5 feet deep. You may set 4×4 posts into the ground and nail the wall boards to the posts. The bins shown have 1×6 skids at the ends and dividers, so you can tow them with a garden tractor.

SIMPLE ASSEMBLY

Building the bins is simple. Pressure-treated lumber and galvanized fasteners will avoid corrosion and wood rot.

Construct the framework from 1×6s. Space the wall boards with 1×6 spacers to let air flow through. To keep compost from spilling, staple galvanized wire mesh inside the bins.

Build doors with slotted corner and end posts to permit turning and removal of the compost. Slip the 1× boards into the slots, and remove them for tending the compost.

COMPOST BASICS

The important thing to remember when composting is to limit the carbon content of the waste. Use kitchen wastes, for example—they have a low carbon level. So do grass clippings. Fruit wastes are acceptable, but meats, dairy products, and high fat foods are not. Tree leaves, sawdust, and wood are poor candidates for composting.

Keep the waste damp but not wet. Within days, the temperature inside the compost pile will reach 140° to 165° F. If the process seems slow, add high nitrogen fertilizer or commercial compost activators to speed things up.

Three compost bins are needed: One holds finished compost, another bin holds "cooking" compost materials, and the third bin holds fresh vegetable scraps. The doors are 1×6s that can be removed for easy access to the compost.

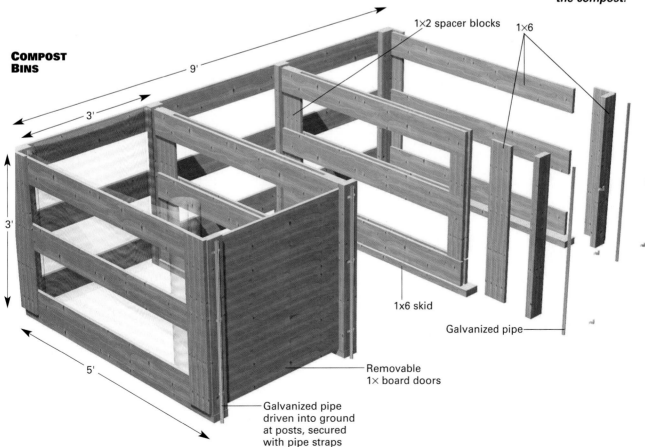

COMPOST BINS

9'

3'

3'

5'

1×2 spacer blocks

1×6

1×6 skid

Galvanized pipe

Removable 1× board doors

Galvanized pipe driven into ground at posts, secured with pipe straps

PONDS

Ponds can make a splash in any dry old patch of landscape. A garden pond adds sparkle to your yard, showcases goldfish and aquatic plants, and lures birds and other wildlife.

MATERIALS

Flexible pond liners have revolutionized the use of water in home landscaping. The liner is a low-cost, easy-to-install, custom-fit alternative to concrete or molded forms. Molded fiberglass ponds come in many sizes and shapes, but you should expect to pay extra for fanciful custom designs.

LAYOUT AND EXCAVATION

A vinyl liner keeps this pond full and clear; use rocks or patio blocks to conceal the edges. Garden centers also offer rigid plastic pools in various sizes and shapes.

Outline the pond shape on the lawn with a garden hose. Next, remove the sod and excavate to a depth of 9 inches, sloping the sides at about a 20-degree angle. Leave a ledge—a shelf for aquatic plants—then dig again to a total pond depth of 18 inches. Slope this final excavation also. Your garden supply center can help you select attractive plants for the ledge.

LEVELING THE EDGE

Level the edge of the pool along its entire perimeter. Center a post in the excavation area and extend a leveled 1×4 from the post to the edge. Mark a horizontal line where the 1×4 intersects the grade.

Dig to this depth around the perimeter of the pond, repositioning the board as you go. Your edging should be at least 2 inches above the lawn grade to prevent lawn runoff from contaminating pond water.

LINING THE POOL

Line the pool bottom with damp sand and spread the liner over the excavation. Press the liner down and add 4 to 6 inches of water. The weight of the water will form the liner to the pool.

Adjust the liner to prevent wrinkles, and fill in increments, adjusting as you go. When the pond is filled, lay flagstone or pavers on the pond edge and cut away the excess liner.

Install a GFCI outlet to power a submersible pump or fountain to circulate and aerate the water.

INSTALLING A POND LINER

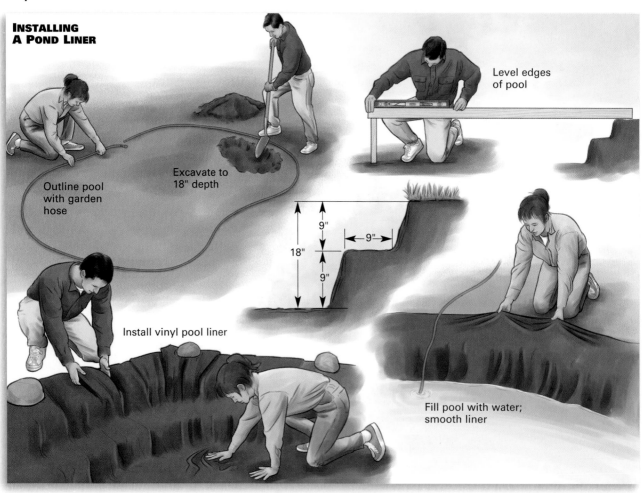

Outline pool with garden hose

Excavate to 18" depth

Level edges of pool

18"   9"   9"   9"

Install vinyl pool liner

Fill pool with water; smooth liner

INDEX

METRIC CONVERSIONS

U.S. Units to Metric Equivalents			Metric Units to U.S. Equivalents		
To Convert From	Multiply By	To Get	To Convert From	Multiply By	To Get
Inches	25.4	Millimeters	Millimeters	0.0394	Inches
Inches	2.54	Centimeters	Centimeters	0.3937	Inches
Feet	30.48	Centimeters	Centimeters	0.0328	Feet
Feet	0.3048	Meters	Meters	3.2808	Feet
Yards	0.9144	Meters	Meters	1.0936	Yards
Square inches	6.4516	Square centimeters	Square centimeters	0.1550	Square inches
Square feet	0.0929	Square meters	Square meters	10.764	Square feet
Square yards	0.8361	Square meters	Square meters	1.1960	Square yards
Acres	0.4047	Hectares	Hectares	2.4711	Acres
Cubic inches	16.387	Cubic centimeters	Cubic centimeters	0.0610	Cubic inches
Cubic feet	0.0283	Cubic meters	Cubic meters	35.315	Cubic feet
Cubic feet	28.316	Liters	Liters	0.0353	Cubic feet
Cubic yards	0.7646	Cubic meters	Cubic meters	1.308	Cubic yards
Cubic yards	764.55	Liters	Liters	0.0013	Cubic yards

To convert from degrees Fahrenheit (F) to degrees Celsius (C), first subtract 32, then multiply by $5/9$.

To convert from degrees Celsius to degrees Fahrenheit, multiply by $9/5$, then add 32.